GW01471587

SUPPORT FOSTER CARE

Developing a short-break service
for children in need

Margaret Greenfields and June Statham

Thomas Coram Research Unit
Institute of Education, University of London

INSTITUTE OF
EDUCATION
UNIVERSITY OF LONDON

Quality Protects

department for
education and skills

First published in 2004 by the Institute of Education, University of London,
20 Bedford Way, London WC1H 0AL

Over 100 years of excellence in education

© Institute of Education, University of London 2004

British Library Cataloguing in Publication Data:
A catalogue record for this publication is available from the British Library

ISBN 0 85473 697 2

This work was undertaken by the Thomas Coram Research Unit, which receives
support from the Department of Health; the views expressed in this publication are
those of the authors and not necessarily those of the Department of Health or the
Department for Education and skills.

Design by Tim McPhee
Page make-up by Cambridge Photosetting Services

Production services by
Book Production Consultants plc, Cambridge

Printed by Black Bear Press, Cambridge

Contents

List of tables and figures

Acknowledgements

The authors would like to thank the Department of Health for funding the Support Care study, and all the local authority staff who participated in the survey and telephone interviews. We are very grateful to the support carers who gave up their precious free time to share their experiences of providing short breaks for children in need, and in particular to the co-ordinators of the three case study schemes, who provided us with a wealth of additional information and were extremely generous with their time. Ena Fry of Fostering Network and Joy Howard of Bradford Support Care gave invaluable assistance in identifying local authorities with support care schemes. We would also like to thank Annabelle Stapleton at the Thomas Coram Research Unit for her administrative support for this project.

1 Introductory summary

Background

Under section 20 of the Children Act 1989, local authorities can provide short breaks for children with foster or other families. The majority of such placements are used to support the families of disabled children, but they may also be used in other circumstances. Support foster care schemes aim to work with families who are experiencing difficulties or stress by providing this type of short break for children and support for parents. Such schemes have been slow to develop, and the Department of Health commissioned the Thomas Coram Research Unit to carry out a small-scale study to find out more about the barriers, legal and otherwise, that might be deterring local authorities from establishing support care schemes, and how such barriers might be overcome.

About the study

In addition to identifying barriers, the study aimed to provide information on the extent of support care schemes and how they operate; to examine the motivation and views of foster carers who provide this service; and to explore the potential for childminders to offer this kind of short-break support to families in the light of recent changes in the regulation of childminding. Information was obtained from a variety of sources. A short screening questionnaire was sent to all English local authorities; telephone interviews were undertaken with key officers in 14 authorities, both with and without support care schemes; three schemes were studied in more depth (work included focus groups with support carers); and co-ordinators of community childminding networks were surveyed. The fieldwork was carried out between March and August 2003.

Key findings

Only a small number of authorities, probably no more than a dozen, currently operate formal support care schemes. However, many offer short breaks to a small number of non-disabled children on an ad hoc basis, usually using existing foster carers, and there is interest in developing further this kind of support for families.

The schemes included in the study varied considerably in size and scope, but all were able to offer a flexible response depending on families' needs. This often involved providing a weekend break every fortnight or month, but could also involve care in the daytime (for example, when children were excluded from school), overnight stays during the week, or short periods of full-time care (for example when a parent needed repeated stays in hospital).

Support care was often used alongside other social work support, and was usually offered for no more than six to nine months.

The majority of support care schemes are currently located within fostering services, but there is a strong case for considering a base within family support services, while maintaining strong links with fostering and family placement teams. Whatever the location, support care needs to be presented to families in a non-stigmatising way and made readily available.

The most frequently mentioned barrier to developing support care schemes was the priority given to 'mainstream' fostering and a fear of possible competition for resources and potential carers. However, the study found that support carers were usually drawn from a pool of people who would not be available for full-time fostering, or who would otherwise have left the fostering service. Providing opportunities for part-time fostering could actually draw in people who might later move on to offer full-time care, as well as keeping other foster carers within the service.

Another barrier was the lower priority often accorded to preventative services. Many schemes had struggled to keep going financially, and had only been able to develop through tapping into additional sources of funding such as Sure Start or grants provided under the Choice Protects initiative. Strong management backing for support care schemes was an important factor in their success.

Legal issues, such as whether children receiving support care needed to be treated as looked after under section 20 of the Children Act, were rarely mentioned as a barrier to setting up schemes, but they did become more of an issue once schemes were operating. There was widespread confusion and varying practice with regard to the need for reviews, medicals and care plans for children receiving support care. Most schemes had decided to operate some form of 'slimmed down' Looking After Children procedures, but were unsure of the legality of this. All authorities reported that they would welcome clarification and guidance from the government in this area.

Support carers were very committed to providing a positive experience for the children placed with them. However, there was general dissatisfaction with the poor pay and increasing pressure to accept more challenging children, and a feeling that the service is marginalised within social services departments.

Some community childminding networks have started to explore the potential to offer a similar short-break service (including overnight care), and there are examples of successful practice. Such schemes operate under different regulations, with no requirement for child-minders to be registered as foster carers.

Although there was little 'hard' evidence of effectiveness because of a lack of monitoring or comparative studies, the available evidence suggests that providing short breaks for children in need helps them to remain with their families and may avoid longer-term care. The service is highly valued by parents, and its flexibility is a particular strength. Short breaks can also provide continuity and stability for children when used alongside periods of accommodation.

Overall, the study suggests there is a need for a more integrated approach to providing this kind of support to families, both at a local authority level (locating support care firmly within a spectrum of services to children and families) and at a national level (for example, greater dialogue between the regulatory bodies responsible for childminding and for foster care). Areas that local authorities need to consider when developing support care services are discussed in Chapter 8, and the appendix (page 51) provides further information on relevant legal issues.

2 Background to the study

A series of short-term pre-planned placements of children in out-of-home care (often called 'family link placements' or 'short breaks') can be provided by local authorities under Section 20 of the Children Act 1989 in order to support families who are experiencing difficulties and stress. The legal requirements for such short-term accommodation are set out in Regulation 13 of the *Guidance and Regulations* in relation to family placement that accompanies the Children Act 1989 (Department of Health 1991). They stipulate that no single placement can be for more than four weeks, the total duration in a year must not exceed 90 days, and all placements must be with the same carer. Statistics collected by the Department of Health indicate that some 12,200 children received such placements during 2001/2 (Department of Health 2003), although there are doubts about the accuracy of these figures.[1] Of these, 11,000 were looked after exclusively under short-term placements, the remaining 1,200 having also been looked after during the year in placements that were not part of an agreed series.

The majority of these placements were to support the families of disabled children, but 28 per cent of children were recorded as being looked after in this way for reasons other than disability, mostly because their parents or carers needed relief. The number of children looked after under a series of short-term placements appeared to rise between 1995 and 1999 but has since been declining, although this may simply reflect incomplete recording of such children in earlier years.

In 2003, the Department of Health commissioned the Thomas Coram Research Unit to undertake a study of support foster care, a particular form of short-term accommodation for children in need, which aims to work with families to support them at times of stress and to enable children to remain at home. Defining characteristics of support foster care are:

- the parent(s) remain the main carer for the child
- the foster carer may provide planned/unplanned care on a day care and/or overnight basis, individually negotiated with the family
- support is provided by the foster carer to the family as well as to the individual child, possibly including when the child is not being cared for by the carer
- it is generally a time-limited scheme, conceived as supporting the family through a difficult time.

Support care[2] could be used in a variety of situations: for example, to provide support to children, young people and their families at times of crisis; to provide a part-time base for young runaways, care leavers and young offenders; or to support kinship care placements by offering regular breaks. It has the potential to prevent a drift into care and to assist with adoption stability. A number of examples are described in research undertaken as part of the Children Act research programme (for example, Aldgate and Bradley 1999; Packman and Hall 1999: 171–2), and a more detailed account of the development of a pioneering scheme in Bradford is given by Howard (1997; 2000). These studies highlight common characteristics of support foster care placements, such as an emphasis on accommodation being a form of family support and a strong focus on working in partnership with parents.

Relatively little is known about the views and experience of part-time foster carers who provide children with short breaks – why they do it, whether they would be prepared to foster full time, how much training and support they receive. Aldgate and Bradley found that all the short-term carers they consulted were motivated by a desire to help children under stress, and almost half also wanted to help parents under stress – often because of their own experiences of loss or disruption, which had made them realise what a difference support could make at such times. A study of short-break carers who provided respite care for disabled children (Tarleton 2003) found that the carers did this work because they enjoyed it and developed real relationships with the children, but that they had concerns about the way in which they were trained, paid and supported by their schemes, which were often related to a lack of staff time and resources and a lack of clarity regarding their role.

The Choice Protects initiative, a three-year review of fostering and placement services announced in 2002, aims to develop a more flexible and extensive range of placement options that work to keep children with their families and help parents to manage their children. Support care could potentially make an important contribution to this aim. Many councils are also experiencing significant difficulties over maintaining an adequate supply of foster carers (Social Services Inspectorate 2002), and offering the possibility of part-time work may well help to address recruitment and retention problems. Despite this, support care schemes have been slow to develop. In early 2003, it was estimated that there were probably no more than a dozen such schemes fully operational across England, although others were known to be 'in the pipeline' (Fry 2003). Some schemes have closed: for example, a personal communication with the Bradford support care co-ordinator revealed that of the four schemes included in the Aldgate and Bradley study, only one was still running in 2003.

Uncertainty on a number of points may be deterring local authorities from establishing support care schemes. These could include:

- the legal status of children within the scheme; the scheme may not sit easily within the distinctions drawn by local authorities between 'voluntary accommodation' under Section 20 of the Children Act 1989 and 'family support' provided under the powers of Section 17
- the perception that, if a child becomes 'looked after' through participation in a support care scheme, the council is subsequently required to apply full benefits (review, care plan, health plan, Personal Education Plan, advocacy etc), even though the child may only be staying away from home on an infrequent basis
- the possibility that the support carers may need to go through a full foster care approval process to accept children for the occasional overnight stay.

Childminders and support care

Some support care schemes are known to recruit carers from their existing pool of foster carers, especially those who no longer wish to care for children full time. Others use registered childminders, who may then be required to be registered as foster carers before they can provide overnight care. However, new arrangements for childminding introduced by Ofsted in 2001 (Department for Education and Skills 2001) allow childminders to be registered to provide overnight care for up to six children under eight years old, for periods up to 27 days, and to offer overnight care for over-eights. This might lead to an extended role for existing community or 'sponsored' childminding schemes, which often support parents as well as providing daytime care for children in need (Statham *et al.* 2000). From April 2003, a new category of childminder, called a 'home childcarer', was also created, registered by Ofsted to work in the child's own home. Little is currently known about how these regulatory changes are operating, and where schemes developed under these provisions might fit or overlap with support care.

Objectives of the study

The TCRU study aimed to:

- provide information on the extent and nature of support foster care schemes in English local authorities, including their objectives and ways of working with children and families
- investigate the legal or other barriers to establishing such schemes
- explore the solutions that authorities were devising for themselves, or wishing to see introduced, to overcome these barriers, and identify any common themes
- investigate the potential impact of changes in the regulation of childminding and home care on the development of support foster care schemes
- examine the motivation and views of foster carers who provide a support care service
- as far as possible, obtain information on the costs of operating a support foster care scheme and compare this with the costs of other 'traditional' foster care schemes
- consider whether there is any evidence that the support care approach produces good outcomes for the family and child in terms of secure attachment to carers.

Methods

The fieldwork for the study took place between March and August 2003 and involved a number of methods and stages.

Questionnaire to local authorities

A short screening questionnaire was sent to all 150 councils with social services responsibilities in England, which aimed to establish whether a support foster care scheme existed or was planned, and asked about barriers and difficulties that had been experienced or would be anticipated in setting one up. Contact details were also requested for the person who could best provide further information. The form was sent with the weekly electronic bulletin to chief executives from the Association of Directors of Social Services in April 2003. After a reminder several weeks later, replies were received from 46 councils (a response rate of 31 per cent). It subsequently emerged that the form had not always been passed on to the relevant person. We therefore used additional methods (see Chapter 3) to identify authorities with support care schemes.

Telephone interviews with local authorities

From the screening survey and other sources, 14 councils were identified: six with an established support care scheme, two in the process of setting up such a scheme, and six who reported in the screening survey that they did not have a support care scheme. They covered a range of local authority types and geographical areas (see Table 2.1). Semi-structured telephone interviews were carried out with up to three individuals in each council: the nominated contact, a senior manager in the family placement or fostering team (where this differed from the nominated contact), and a legal officer where possible and appropriate (for example, if the manager reported particular issues around the legal status of children using support care schemes). Interviews with scheme co-ordinators lasted on average two hours and those with managers in councils without schemes around one hour, while the interviews with legal advisers were shorter, at around 30 minutes. All interviews were tape recorded and written up in a standard format, and the information was then transferred to charts to facilitate the identification of common themes and issues.

The interviews investigated in more depth the difficulties experienced in setting up and/or keeping schemes going, the reasons why authorities without schemes did not have them, and what had or would prove helpful in overcoming barriers to developing a support foster care service. Managers' views were sought about the factors that facilitate or hinder the use of short-term breaks as a family support service, and the authority's practice in applying Looking After Children (LAC) procedures to this form of care. Information was also collected on the costs of support care schemes compared to mainstream fostering, so far as those that were interviewed were able to provide these details.

Case studies in local authorities

Three of the six authorities with well-established support foster care schemes of different types (for example, using foster carers or childminders) were visited and studied in more depth. All three schemes were currently based in family support services, but two had originally been set up within fostering services. This allowed an exploration of issues concerning service location. Information was obtained from face-to-face interviews with scheme managers/co-ordinators and analysis of relevant documentation, including annual reports, planning memos and forms for referral, planning and review. A focus group of six or seven support carers was convened in each of the three case study authorities, lasting from two to three hours. These discussions were tape recorded and subsequently transcribed for analysis.

It was not possible within the timescale and resources of this short study to obtain first-hand information from the users (parents or children) of support care schemes. We did, however, ask scheme co-ordinators and carers to provide feedback on how parents and children responded to the service. Further information on how children perceived short-term breaks can be found in the study by Aldgate and Bradley (1999), which included interviews with both parents and children using short-break fostering schemes.

In total, interviews were conducted with nine senior managers working in fostering or child and family services, seven support care scheme co-ordinators and six legal advisers. The focus groups involved 20 support carers (Table 2.1).

Telephone interviews with childminding schemes and survey of networks

The co-ordinators of six community childminding schemes providing care for children in need, who had been interviewed in 1997 or 1998 as part of an earlier TCRU study of sponsored day care, were re-contacted. Telephone interviews explored the likely impact of the new Ofsted arrangements allowing childminders to provide overnight and home care, and the potential for community childminding schemes to develop into support care work. A short questionnaire was also included in a regular newsletter sent by the National

Table 2.1: Interviews completed

	Local authority type	Senior manager	Scheme co-ordinator	Legal adviser	Carers (in focus groups)
Established scheme					
Authority A	**M**	√	√	√	√ (7)
Authority B	**M**	√	√	√	√ (6)
Authority C	**U**		√ *	√	√ (7)
Authority D	LB		√		
Authority E	M		√ *		
Authority F	U		√ *		
Setting up scheme					
Authority G	U		√ *		
Authority H	SC	√			
No scheme					
Authority J	LB	√		√	
Authority K	U	√			
Authority L	SC	√		√	
Authority M	SC	√			
Authority N	U	√		√	
Authority P	U	√			
Total		9	7	6	20

Key

M   metropolitan
LB   London borough
U   unitary
SC   shire county
*   person interviewed had discussed questions to be asked with a senior manager (e.g. head of children's services) and was providing a joint response

Authorities in bold are case studies

Childminding Association (NCMA) to co-ordinators of childminding networks. These are organisations that bring together childminders in a local area to improve standards and provide support and training. The questionnaire asked about the number of childminders in the network who were registered to provide overnight care, whether any offered short breaks for children in need, if this was a service the network would want to develop, and whether there were any difficulties that would have to be overcome. Responses were received, either electronically or by post, from co-ordinators of 31 networks, representing both rural and urban areas.

Ethical considerations

The study followed the ethical procedures of the Thomas Coram Research Unit, in particular regarding confidentiality and the provision of sufficient information about the study to obtain participants' informed consent. Thomas Coram Research Unit's research procedures are consistent with the requirements of the Data Protection Act 1998.

Report structure

The rest of this report is structured in six main chapters. Chapter 3 provides a broad overview of the extent and nature of support care schemes, looking at how they have developed, where they are located within the range of council provision, the nature of the service offered and the schemes' approach to working with children and parents. Chapter 4 considers barriers to developing schemes, including legal considerations, recruitment of carers, financial and resource issues and the priority given to preventative work within children's social services. Chapter 5 presents information, so far as we were able to obtain this, on the costs and outcomes of support care schemes, while Chapter 6 discusses the motivations and experience of support care workers. Chapter 7 considers the potential for childminders working within childminding networks to provide this kind of short-break service (including overnight care). The final chapter summarises the findings of the study in relation to a number of key questions, and identifies the factors that would facilitate the development of a short-break service for children in need.

1. The figures are based on a one-third sample return. Authorities differ in the way they record these series of short-term placements, and the distinction between these children and others looked after under Section 20 of the Children Act (voluntary accommodation) is known to cause difficulties when recording data for the SSDA903 return. In addition, some authorities may fail to record these children, incorrectly treating them as not looked after.
2. In the rest of this report, we use the term 'support care' rather than 'support foster care', as this was the term preferred by most of the schemes in the study.

3 | The extent and nature of support care schemes

The extent of schemes: survey analysis

In order to obtain information on the extent of support care schemes, a short screening questionnaire was sent to all 150 councils with social services responsibilities in England. The questionnaire defined the key characteristics of a support foster care scheme (see Chapter 2) and asked councils whether they operated such a scheme or had done so in the past, and what barriers they had experienced or would anticipate in setting one up.

Of the 46 councils responding, 12 indicated that they operated a support care scheme and 34 that they did not. One of the 34 indicated that they had run a scheme in the past that had since closed. However, over a quarter of those without a scheme commented that they did provide short-break support on an informal basis to some families (not only those with disabled children), although they did not have a 'scheme' as such. This was confirmed when we interviewed managers in authorities that had reported no scheme. Most had a category of 'respite' foster carers who would occasionally offer short breaks to families directly, as well as to other foster carers.

To complicate the picture further, follow-up telephone calls to the 12 councils in the survey who reported having a scheme established that three in fact mainly offered respite to foster carers who had long-term or particularly challenging placements, rather than short breaks for children living at home. Two were family-link type schemes restricted to disabled children; and two schemes were still in the process of being developed and had not yet begun to offer placements.

Given the initial difficulty of identifying councils with schemes from the survey, help was requested from the Fostering Network, which is actively involved in promoting support care schemes, and the co-ordinator of the Bradford Support Care scheme, an early pioneer in this field who has been developing a national network of contacts. Using these sources of information, enough projects were eventually identified to meet the target for the next stage of the study of six authorities with an established support care scheme. Interestingly, several councils where schemes were believed to operate were no longer running their projects following a change of personnel, or were in a state of abeyance following funding cutbacks or reorganisation of responsibilities within the authority. It was apparent that schemes often suffered from a lack of continuity and a struggle to maintain funding, a theme that recurred throughout the study.

The screening survey showed that, among councils which offer short breaks on an ad hoc basis, there is a definite interest in further development of support care for families. Two councils reported definite plans to set up schemes, and four that they were currently exploring the possibility of doing so. The telephone interviews undertaken in the second part of this study with councils that did not have support care schemes also resulted in a number of interviewees noting that they would now consider the need and potential for such projects, and think about how they could be developed in their own area.

The nature of schemes: interview data

Six local authorities with schemes were identified for the second stage of the research, plus two that were in the process of developing this service. Key characteristics are summarised in Table 3.1. This chapter provides an overview of these schemes, drawing on information from in-depth telephone interviews with managers or project co-ordinators. Additional information was obtained in the three case study areas (authorities A, B and C) from face-to-face interviews, analysis of documents and a focus group of carers. The two authorities that were developing schemes (G and H) were at different stages and not able to provide all the information we needed. One had recently begun recruiting potential carers and was still working on devising procedures for the project; the other had just completed a pilot phase of the scheme and had one carer who had recently completed her first placement. Where applicable, we have included information from all eight schemes in the information presented below.

Development of schemes

The eight projects included two early trailblazers, both in metropolitan areas. One of these had developed from a sponsored childminding scheme in 1989, and the other was first proposed in 1992, although it did not become operational until 1996. A 'second wave' of schemes then appeared from the late 1990s, with one project beginning in 1998, three in 1999, and the two schemes under development first receiving funding in 2002 or 2003.

All four of the schemes which commenced in the late 1990s resulted from particular senior management initiatives, usually due to the enthusiasm of a particular individual in response to concerns about the lack of preventative services in the area and an increase in looked after children.

> There were a lot of repeat referrals. Families coming in and asking for support, fairly low-level stuff, but because there weren't any preventative service there, they were being fobbed off and because they weren't getting any services it was coming back at a far higher level. It might come back in as a child protection matter or children needing to be accommodated.
>
> (Project manager, Authority C)

This gap in family support services had also been identified by the carers and staff who initiated the early schemes. The childminders in Authority A, who at the end of the 1980s were providing daytime-only care for children referred by social services, had reported that 'lots of families are saying if only we could have the children overnight, or if only we could have them at weekends'.

In contrast, the two schemes that were currently being developed had been proposed as a way of avoiding the breakdown of mainstream fostering placements by providing respite services to carers, but their co-ordinators were now considering extending the service to parents. In one case, the fostering manager decided to expand the fledging respite care scheme to include supporting children at home when a young person who had been receiving respite care while in a mainstream fostering placement was being returned to relative care. It was felt that this young person's rehabilitation to home would fail without additional support. In the other authority, an audit of needs and services had suggested that

Table 3.1: Overview of schemes

Local Authority	Date set up	Location	Support carers	Children placed	Service provided
A	1989	Family Support	7 (+ 1 being assessed)	Approx 100 per year	Childminders with dual registration as foster carers provide short-term support (generally lasting around 3 months) to families with children aged 0–8. May be day care, evenings or overnight stays, e.g. 2 days a week or 2 weekends a month. Occasionally short periods of full-time care are offered (max 7 consecutive nights).
B	1996	Family Support	23	142 children placed in 2002/03. Approx 70 families at any one time	Placements tailored to needs of individual family, commonly one weekend a month or 1 or 2 schooldays especially if child excluded from school. Usually last 6–9 months.
C	1998	Family Support	17	Currently supporting 51 children + 5 introductions + 3 emergency placements	Flexible service; may be 48 hour block midweek or alternate weekends. Occasionally provides in-home support e.g. for teenage mother. May be time limited or longer term and also provides periods of short-term full-time care and emergency placements.
D	1999	Fostering	10	N/A	Usually 1 weekend a month, with most carers having 2 placements and thus working 2 weekends per month. Mostly 6 months max, but 'not set in stone'. Focus on activities with children/young people (e.g. swimming, sports); recreation allowance is provided.
E	1999	Fostering	5 (+ 3 mainstream who also do short breaks)	Approx 7 placements in 2002 and 2003	Flexibility limited by what carers are able to offer, usually 1 weekend a month. Currently no time limits but may be introduced if scheme expands.
F	1999	Fostering	6 or 7 (+ 3 mainstream)	Approx 8–10 children at any one time	Time limited service combined with other family support. Typically offers 2 sessions/days a month, for 6 months.
G	2002 (pilot)	Fostering	1 (+ 4 being assessed)	1 (supported within family)	Developed as respite service for foster carers but hope to extend to support children living at home.
H	2003 (in development)	Fostering	None yet	None yet	Plans to develop the service initially on lines of Link service for disabled children, which offers up to 30 days per year.

offering respite support to parents could help the authority to avoid accommodating children, and that such a service could be incorporated into the respite provision which was being developed for foster carers.

Staffing and resource issues

The costs of running support care schemes are covered in Chapter 5. However, the adequacy or otherwise of staffing and resources had a significant impact on the way in which schemes had been able to develop and the extent of the service they could offer. The majority of schemes reported that they had experienced significant difficulties in accessing adequate funding to keep their projects running.

> We had to do it on a shoestring and borrow people, beg people's services.
> (Authority A) [no increase in funding from 1992–2002]

> We need to try and offer a reasonable service, but we can't offer a very good service if we don't have the staff and the finances.
>
> (Authority G)

The two most long-standing projects, in particular, had experienced quite lengthy periods of time where their budgets were static, they lacked administrative support, were unable to increase payments to carers and could not offer them any social worker support. These two projects had survived through the tenacity and commitment of the co-ordinators, but other schemes had disappeared. Two recent projects in the study were in fact resurrections of schemes which had operated in the past but which interviewees reported as having become 'moribund' or 'stagnant' through lack of investment and a consequent loss of carers, even though the service had been popular with social workers and families.

Box 1: Support care scheme located within family support

The support care scheme in Authority C has always enjoyed considerable support from managers in both fostering and family support services. It was set up in 1998 following a 'needs and services' review which identified both a need for support services before families reached crisis point, and the importance of services being accessible to families. The views of service users were sought to assist in identifying the most appropriate form of family support provision, and support care was highlighted as a priority, as was the importance of presenting the service in a non-threatening manner. This philosophy has been emphasised still further through a recent relocation to a dedicated family support site. A range of innovative projects are being developed as part of the authority's preventative strategy, including training support carers as family group conference convenors. Both the co-ordinator and the children's services manager identify the location and presentation of the scheme within family support services as being crucial in avoiding the potential stigma of children being seen as 'in care', and in promoting working in partnership with parents.

Another significant factor in the development of schemes had been the support of senior managers. The two long-standing schemes had both experienced various changes of management over the years, and at times had had considerable problems in convincing senior managers of the necessity of funding and supporting their projects. Both now felt their projects were well supported within their authorities, and that their current senior manager was committed to developing support care services. The two recently developed schemes (C and F), which had been relatively well funded and staffed since their inception, both enjoyed a top-down commitment to supporting the project from the start (see Box 1).

A key message which arose from this aspect of the research was the critical importance of strong management backing for support care schemes, and the impact which a well-devised strategy plan and mainstreaming of the service has on both staff morale and the efficiency of service delivery. In cases where co-ordinators had been left to develop a service on a piecemeal, poorly funded basis, it would appear that the service had only survived for any considerable period of time through the dedication of individual staff and carers, who frequently reported a sense of isolation and lack of support from both senior management and other departments within the authority.

The service offered

The schemes included in the study varied considerably in size and scope. The three case study authorities offered support care to 100 or more children a year, but the others operated on a much smaller scale (Table 3.1). One scheme (a pilot project) had only one carer; another had over 20.

A key characteristic of the established support care schemes was their flexibility to respond in a variety of ways depending on the needs of the child and family. Weekend breaks were particularly common, either once a month or once a fortnight, but support carers also offered care during the daytime (especially to preschool-aged children and those excluded from school) and regular overnight stays during the week. One carer, for example, took two teenage girls on Monday evenings, a boy on Tuesday evenings, and another boy for a full weekend once a month. Full-time care could also be offered for short periods, enabling tailor-made packages of care to be created for children whose families had longer term needs. In one example, the children of a mother with a cyclical mental health problem were provided with support care for one weekend a month, but were also able to spend longer periods of time with the carer when their mother had to be hospitalised.

Although the pattern of care offered varied according to the availability of carers and the needs of the family, most support care schemes had a strong philosophy of time-limited acute service delivery, to discourage parental dependence on the service. Short breaks were typically provided for no more than six to nine months, to help parents 'get back on their feet'. There was also an emphasis on support care as part of a package of support to enable the family to overcome temporary difficulties. This could be work with parents (such as support by social workers or family support workers) or other services for children (such as attendance at a child and adolescent mental health clinic). One scheme co-ordinator explained that 'these things only work if social workers are using the "feel-good" effect to sort of get in and do a piece of work'. Another described how her scheme explicitly excluded families with long-term or chronic needs, and noted that 'if with social services and other sorts of support going in there is no change in six months, then we need to think about ... whether or not a child can be retained at home, as [support care] is part of a whole package'.

The support care approach

Co-ordinators and managers in all eight local authorities offering support care schemes adhered to a common philosophy of working in partnership with parents to avoid long-term accommodation of children. Although in two authorities the initial driver behind developing support care schemes had been concerns over mainstream placements breaking down through lack of respite for foster carers, the decision to extend the service to direct support for families was a recognition that the impact on children and families of 'coming into care' could potentially be avoided by the provision of some form of respite for families under stress, preferably in conjunction with some other form of task-centred, short-term family support. The emphasis in support care was on strengthening families' own ability to cope with their situation.

> If a family can ask for, say, two hours [a week] and that two hours means that family can survive, I think we should do that. If we are empowering that family, then we need to ask that family what they need.
>
> (Co-ordinator, Authority G)

Several interviewees referred to the fact that the actual offer of help could sometimes be enough to help a family, even if the service was not taken up.

> Families can sometimes manage something if they know there is something there [which is] concrete.
>
> (Co-ordinator, Authority D)

Access to support care in the majority of cases involved referral from a social worker, although three co-ordinators noted that they would like to see a wider access policy, with doctors or health visitors being able to refer families directly to the project, rather than asking them to approach their social worker or the duty team to ask for services. The two long-running schemes did accept referrals from health professionals and other agencies, and had not experienced the deluge of requests for help that other authorities, concerned about pressure on resources, sometimes predicted.

> People say if you have an open door policy you are going to be swamped, but it hasn't proved the case.
>
> (Authority B)

> My view is if someone is coming forward to a professional saying, 'I need help,' then they need help … most families I know would steer well clear of social services if they didn't need them.
>
> (Authority A)

Working with parents

An important part of the support care approach was working in partnership with parents. Although this is also the intention behind the provision of voluntary accommodation under Section 20 of the Children Act 1989, the co-ordinator of the scheme in Authority B drew a distinction between this and support care:

> I didn't see [repeat episodes of accommodation] as a partnership at all. I saw it as a parent giving up, the local authority taking over and then just returning the child to the parent.

She went on to spell out the reasons that support care was different:

> What we're trying to do is give parents the message that they have not given up any control, they're the people in the driving seat still with their child, all we're doing is giving them a few breaks to help them, to enable them to do that. We are not taking over any department of their lives.

The definition of support care that was provided to local authorities in our screening survey (derived from the Department of Health's specification for the research project) included the assertion that 'support is provided by the foster carer to the family as well as to the individual child, possibly including when the child is not being cared for by the carer'. In fact, none of the six established schemes in our study expected carers to carry out direct work with parents in their own homes, and co-ordinators stressed that the level of involvement with a parent, and support offered, varied between individual carers.

Co-ordinators most commonly cited 'signposting' of services and 'emotional support' and 'befriending' of parents as the family support functions carried out by support carers. In two cases, professionals noted that because carers were generally local to an area, they were able to advise parents of the whereabouts of community centres, mother and toddler clubs and similar social activities. Co-ordinators generally felt that attending at schools or hospital appointments with a parent would be outside of a carer's remit, but that telephone or face-to-face advice on parenting issues, or simply acting as a 'listening ear', would be an appropriate role.

Carers themselves, however, reported that although they were not explicitly expected to provide family support, they often found themselves providing a significant level of emotional support for parents. Most had found ways of keeping boundaries and discouraging parents from depending upon them too much, although every carer who participated in focus groups spoke of the blurring of boundaries caused by the fact that parents had their home telephone numbers and addresses, and on occasion might simply 'drop by' or phone them up in a crisis.

While carers were generally willing to accept this as part of their role, it was clear that some difficulties could occur if parents began to telephone them on a daily basis, or late in the evening when depressed. Several carers raised the issue of parents becoming dependent upon them (to the extent that one carer found that she had been designated as a guardian of the children in a newly drawn up will). In such cases, carers referred the situation back to their co-ordinator. However, despite the tensions inherent in balancing a professional caring role with that of being a 'befriender' to a parent, carers spoke with genuine warmth of some parents who had thanked them for their support and assistance at times of crisis, or who had simply felt more able to cope with a parenting issue after seeking advice from the carer. One participant recounted an incident where she had spent several hours one evening providing telephone support to a parent who had been suicidal. The parent had later reported that the fact that the carer had taken time to talk her through a crisis had 'saved my life'. There is, however, a potential cause for concern about the stress on carers if they lack clear boundaries of their role in relation to parents.

Location and presentation of the service

Five of the eight support care schemes were located within fostering teams, despite the concerns of some co-ordinators that this might make families anxious or reluctant to use the project because of the potential stigma of approaching a fostering department, or fears that their children would be taken into care. All schemes registered support carers as foster carers, even when the service was based in family support. Concerns over the apparent contradiction between offering a family support service within a fostering context, and the message which this sends to parents, were expressed by all but two co-ordinators in such situations and are discussed further in the next chapter. The two schemes where staff had not raised location as a concern were both predominantly offering respite to mainstream foster carers, and it may be that the issue of service presentation had not yet arisen.

Almost all schemes had initially been set up within the fostering service, for historical and practical reasons (such as the need to register carers as foster carers). Only the project in Authority C was explicitly located within family support services from the time of the scheme's inception, in 1998. The two most long-standing projects had started off in fostering services, but were now located in one case in family support (based in the local Sure Start office) and in the other in the area children's services team. The co-ordinator in Authority A considered that they were now appropriately placed:

> We are actually in a place where we should be finally ... we've always been a bit of a square peg in a round hole before that.

The co-ordinator in Authority B likewise felt that the support care scheme was 'more closely aligned with the ethos of work going on (in family support services)', and that the family social workers 'understood immediately' what the scheme was aiming to achieve, which compared favourably to the lack of interest she had experienced from staff in the fostering service. However, she was also able to identify a number of disadvantages associated with the move away from fostering. These included the fact that payments, training and approval of carers were still controlled by the fostering unit; that it was less easy to recruit new support carers from among mainstream foster carers who might be thinking of leaving the service; that it was necessary to 'keep reminding people that we are here', and that there was a risk that support carers' work could be devalued if it was not seen as part of the foster care continuum.

Most co-ordinators appeared to favour a status midway between fostering and family support, describing their ideal in terms such as 'a hybrid plot in the middle [of family support and fostering]' and 'something in between [outreach teams and fostering]'. Given their concerns over 'user-friendly' presentation of the service to families, it is unsurprising that co-ordinators often avoided using the term 'fostering' in headed paper or literature which might be accessed by service users. They had devised a variety of alternatives. One project referred to itself as 'neighbourhood care', three local authorities presented the service as a 'support care' scheme, and one described it as 'short breaks'. Two areas mitigated the potentially threatening term 'fostering' by adding 'part-time' or 'support' to their titles. The final local authority which was running a scheme simply identified the service by the name of a planet, in line with terminology used to describe a variety of other family support and fostering schemes operating within the area.

Placement procedures

The longer-standing projects had well-developed placement procedures, which fitted well with the philosophy of partnership with parents. Once a family was referred to the service, Looking After Children forms (in some cases modified) would be completed and a carer sought who could meet the family's needs. A number of factors limited the ability of co-ordinators to match families to carers, especially in small schemes. These included insufficient space within some carers' homes to accommodate children overnight, and the fact that most authorities had few support carers from minority ethnic backgrounds.

Co-ordinators placed great stress upon the importance of parent and child agreeing to the placement. In almost all authorities, the placement procedure began with identification of a suitable carer, followed by an informal visit by parents to the carer's home 'to get a feel of what the place is like'. In at least one authority, parents were able to bring a friend with them for support. A family placement visit was then usually arranged where the children were introduced to the potential carer. Either party (carer or family) could refuse a placement after the initial visit, and an attempt would then made to find another carer for the child.

Although a placement agreement was drawn up specifying the duration of service and dates on which care would be offered, in practice almost all co-ordinators and carers noted that some degree of flexibility could occur. The carer and parent might agree to swap a weekend session for a midweek visit (with the co-ordinator's approval), or social workers might ask carers to vary the agreed arrangements in order to facilitate some other piece of task-focused work with the family, or to give a stressed parent a period of respite earlier than had been planned.

Profile of service users

Most schemes provided short breaks for children and young people of all ages, although one project which had initially begun as a sponsored childminding scheme was available to children under eight. Four of the six established schemes reported that the majority of service users were white, working-class, lone parent mothers with several children. Apart from the scheme focusing on under eights, referrals most commonly concerned boys between the ages of nine and 13, often living with single mothers. The figures provided by Authority B, which kept good records of service users, illustrate a typical pattern (Figure 3.1).

Figure 3.1: Support care placements 2001/2, by age and gender (Authority B)

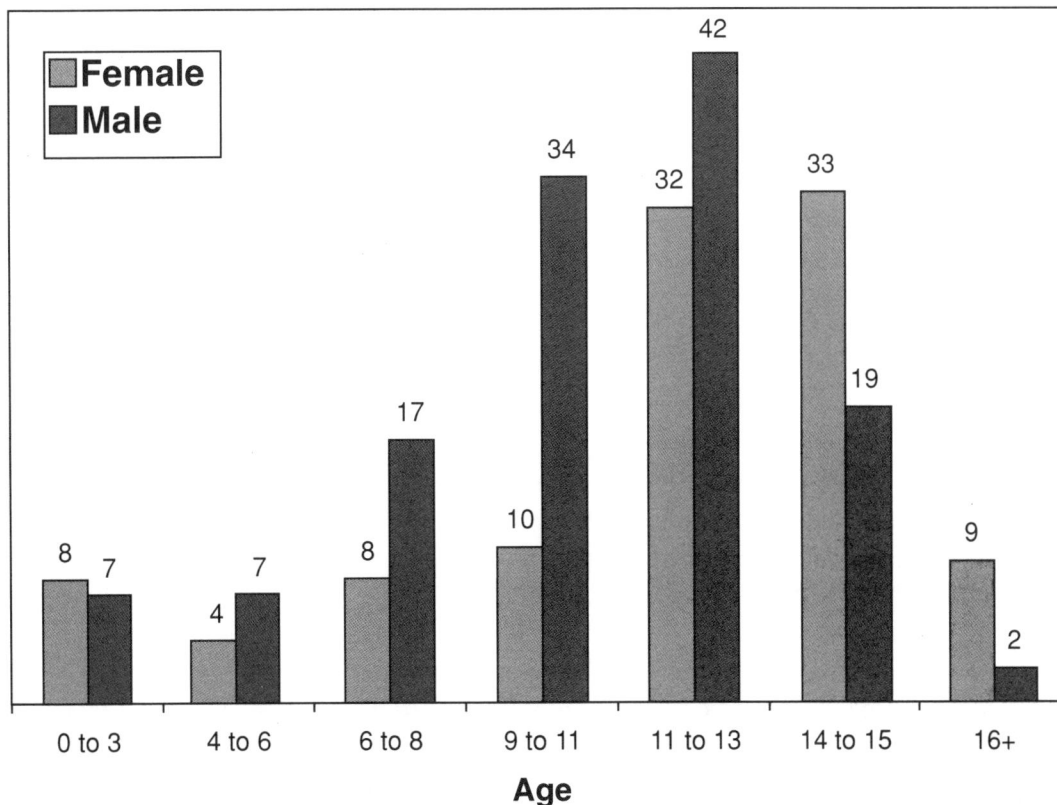

Parents using services were mostly unemployed. Some were in step-parenting relationships where difficulties existed between children and stepfathers, and several professionals noted using support care for parents with mental health problems suffering social isolation and lack of family support networks. Despite the number of referrals relating to parental/adolescent conflict, three co-ordinators referred to the difficulties they experienced in placing teenagers. Four co-ordinators noted that older children tended to be reluctant to take up respite placements; they had 'their own friends and social life' or 'voted with their feet'.

Only two schemes reported any placements of non-White children, and in one of these the high proportion of Black children receiving support care reflected the population mix in the local area. In the other area, the majority of placements concerned White families, but some 'mixed race' children had also used the service. Two co-ordinators noted the infrequency of referrals for members of Asian communities, and suggested that the close-knit nature of these communities meant that families tended not to approach social services departments for family support services. Several mentioned the need to put more effort into recruiting carers from a range of minority ethnic backgrounds, and do more to publicise the service in minority ethnic communities.

Five co-ordinators referred explicitly to the value of support care in stabilising kinship care placements – especially where a grandparent was raising a child, and lack of a break meant that the primary placement was being placed under considerable stress. Places were also increasingly being requested for children with challenging behaviour, such as autistic spectrum and Attention Deficit Hyperactivity Disorder (ADHD). The particular demands that this placed on support carers are discussed further in Chapter 6.

Future developments

In general, all eight co-ordinators were positive about the future of their projects, although in the smaller schemes with limited staff capacities, concerns were noted about the stress on social workers if greater numbers of carers were recruited who required support and training in evenings and weekends. This problem was particularly acute where workers were also expected to manage a mainstream fostering (or other family support) workload on a part-time basis.

Scheme co-ordinators had many plans for how their projects could be developed in the future, illustrating the potential flexibility of this kind of short-break service. Ideas included:

- greater support for kinship carers
- links to remand fostering schemes
- working with young runaways
- working with children excluded from school
- a 'buddying' scheme for young people at risk of social exclusion, including care leavers and teenage parents
- post-adoption support
- training carers as family group conference convenors
- expanding the support care scheme across the authority in partnership with the health authority.

4 Barriers to developing support care schemes

A key concern of the study was to identify the barriers that might be preventing local authorities from developing support care services. This chapter draws on information from both the screening survey and the interviews to explore the difficulties that established schemes had experienced and the potential barriers envisaged by authorities without schemes. More detailed information about the legal status of children receiving support care, based on the views of a sample of legal advisers, is contained in Appendix 1.

Survey analysis

Of the 46 councils responding to the screening survey, 16 did not mention any specific barriers to developing a support care scheme (Table 4.1). Three of these authorities already had a scheme, and a further nine were considering developing one. Of the 30 councils that described one or more barriers, by far the most frequently mentioned (by almost two thirds) was the priority placed on recruiting carers for the mainstream fostering service, and a fear that support care schemes might create competition for an increasingly scarce resource. This was not in fact upheld by the experience of existing schemes, as shown later in this chapter, but there remained a perception that the most urgent task was to recruit and retain full-time foster carers, and that the difficulties most councils were experiencing in this area prohibited using carers in a more flexible way, or diverting resources into recruiting carers specifically for short-break work.

A second perceived barrier was lack of resources, including funding for the additional support and training that would be needed by carers who were supporting parents. A related resource issue was the anticipated impact on workloads for fostering team staff and management; and the difficulty of exploring new ideas and setting up new initiatives given current staffing pressures. Uncertainty about where a support care scheme would fit into the range of services offered by the council was raised by several respondents, who felt it would sit more happily in a family support than a fostering context. One noted that 'it seems a different task from mainstream fostering', another was concerned about potential overlap with the job of family support workers.

Other perceived barriers included anticipated difficulty in attracting carers with the necessary skills (for example, the ability to work with parents), uncertainty about appropriate payment levels for part-time carers, and the potential for misuse of the scheme, either by social workers (who, it was feared, would find it difficult to accept time-limited placements), or by parents who might refuse to have children back home (Table 4.1). One respondent explained that this kind of service had not been developed because there had been 'no explicit demand' from child and family social workers, while acknowledging that it would undoubtedly be welcomed. Another, small, authority was reluctant to pursue numerous specialist fostering schemes and thought it better to make flexible use of main-stream carers for this kind of work instead.

Legal issues, such as whether children receiving support care needed to be counted as looked after, were not mentioned by survey respondents as a barrier to setting up schemes. However, such issues did figure in the subsequent telephone interviews, especially the interviews with co-ordinators of existing schemes, who were in some cases finding that lack of clarity over children's legal status was hindering the development of their work.

Table 4.1: Barriers to establishing a support care scheme (survey)

Barrier	Number of councils mentioning (out of 46)
Shortage of carers/priority to mainstream fostering	19
Resources and funding	10
Staff workloads	8
Skills needed	5
Appropriate location for service	4
Payment issues	3
Potential misuse of scheme	3
No demand	1
Schemes too inflexible	1
No specific barriers mentioned	16

The following discussion on perceived barriers to setting up support foster care schemes draws upon interview material from co-ordinators (and, in three cases, managers) from 14 local authorities: six with schemes, six without, and two in the process of developing projects.

Legal barriers

Most scheme co-ordinators/managers believed that support care needed to be provided under Section 20 (s20) of the Children Act 1989, and had received legal advice that this was the case. One authority was exploring the option of placing children under Section 17 (s17) following the recent LAC (2003) 13 guidance on provision of accommodation to children in need, but this proposal was subject to some resistance by the authority's legal department (see Appendix).

Becoming looked after

All of the authorities that had support care schemes, or were in the process of setting them up, provided this service under s20 of the Children Act. However, the majority of scheme co-ordinators would have preferred this not to be the case. They expressed concerns about requiring children to be treated as looked after, both because of the potential to alienate parents and because of the extensive paperwork required when a child becomes accommo-dated. In some cases, families had declined to take up a placement as a result of the stigma associated with looked after status. In addition, where local authorities insisted that children have a medical prior to placement (in line with usual s20 placement rules), families were often reluctant to take their child to their own GP, who would then know that they were accessing social services support. Children themselves could also regard the requirement for a medical as traumatic and unnecessary in order to receive the occasional weekend break.

> The medical is a huge [problem] …some families drop out the minute you mention it.
>
> (Co-ordinator, Authority A)

When asked whether families might be more willing to accept support foster care if it could be accessed via s17, four co-ordinators felt strongly that offering the service in such a manner would improve accessibility, and that families might prove more willing to approach social services for help before reaching crisis point.

> If the Department of Health [were to] say you can categorise them under s17 I would be absolutely delighted with that … because it is a family support service for children in need and they are not looked after children in that sense. It would remove some of the stigma for parents who feel that it isn't care.
>
> (Manager, Authority B)

In contrast, two scheme co-ordinators felt that while families might approach the service at an earlier stage if it was seen as s17 help, they were not sure that any great difference in profile or take-up would occur, as families were generally fairly desperate by the time they had accessed support care. They also expressed concerns about the way in which placements would be regulated if they were not made under s20. The remaining two interviewees emphasised that families needed a non-stigmatising service provided by sympathetic staff and carers, regardless of whether or not the service was accessed under s20 or s17.

> I don't think families know whether it's s17 support or whatever else it is. What they want is a service where they're going to feel respected and where they're going to be allowed to work through their problems but still feel in control. These are some of the things that parents have said in evaluations … so although it is 'care' it isn't perceived of as care, it's perceived of as helpful, friendly.
>
> (Co-ordinator, Authority B)

Looking After Children documentation

Six interviewees (five co-ordinators and one manager) also reported that they considered that Looking After Children (LAC) paperwork was 'unwieldy' or 'inappropriate' for support care, and that social work staff referring families to the scheme were reluctant to follow full procedures, such as visits and reviews of placements, when a child was only accommodated for occasional days.

> [LAC forms] are still too cumbersome and give the wrong message.
>
> (Co-ordinator, Authority B)

> It really doesn't sit well that I have to explain for purely technical purposes we are accommodating this child.
>
> (Co-ordinator, Authority E)

In the light of the widespread dissatisfaction with having to use LAC paperwork for support care, several authorities had sought legal advice on the possibility of modifying or dispensing with certain elements of the LAC procedures for children receiving short breaks. Three co-ordinators and managers reported that they had received widely conflicting legal and policy advice on their ability to adapt paperwork for support care schemes, and that a need existed for the Department of Health to clarify the minimum recording and procedural requirements for such projects.

Each authority appeared to have devised their own interpretations of LAC paperwork requirements for support care schemes. Two authorities simply fulfilled all LAC requirements, including medicals, reviews and so on. Another scheme completed 'all the initial paperwork', but only reviewed placements if a child became accommodated on a longer-term basis, and also dispensed with medicals. In still another interpretation, the Essential Information Record Part I, Placement Plan Part II and in-house review documents were used. A medical was not required, but reviews occurred after three months of sessions, which could mean after just three weekends of care. Co-ordinators of three well-established projects reported that they had modified the paperwork to dispense with medicals, adapted or dispensed with care plans, and carried out an informal review at around three months.

It was clear that some clarification and guidance on suitable amendments to LAC paperwork would be welcomed by authorities, to limit the confusion and potential for legal error, as well as wasted staff time inherent in the current piecemeal development of tailor-made documentation. As one co-ordinator noted, 'in the absence of any clear guidance from the DH, we are just having to make it up'.

Guidance might also encourage authorities without support care schemes to consider setting them up. When we asked managers in six authorities without schemes how they would go about developing such a service, there was some confusion about what would be required in the way of paperwork and children's legal status. Three managers thought that they would base a scheme for providing short breaks for children in need on existing Link schemes for disabled children, using similarly modified LAC paperwork and procedures (different reviews, plans, fewer meetings and so on). However, not all were sure that they were currently following the correct procedures for Link scheme placements.

Two managers whose authorities did not currently offer support care, but who were actively engaged in devising innovative family support initiatives, considered that it might be possible to 'safely circumvent' LAC procedures by creating a new category of foster carer. This person would meet all of the Fostering Services Regulations 2002, but be similar in status to either a family support worker or a kinship carer (again, this is described further in the Appendix). It was suggested that if such a solution could be devised (through extending policies currently under development) a child would only become looked after if they were 'living with' a carer. The manager of one of these authorities would particularly welcome DH advice on when children *must* be accommodated in order to stay overnight or 'live' with family support carers.

Recording support care statistics

Recording children receiving support care as looked after could have an adverse impact on placement stability and LAC indicators. This was mentioned by three interviewees:

> One of the things that was said to me is, 'If you put down short breaks it counts as too many moves, and that is a negative.'
>
> (Co-ordinator, Authority E)

Similarly, concerns were noted by several co-ordinators that recording all children receiving support care under s20 could make the LAC statistics 'go through the roof', a factor which carried considerable disincentives given performance targets to lower the numbers of looked after children.

> We want to develop this scheme, but if [children receiving support care] are counted as LAC we are shooting ourselves in the foot because we've got to bring down the number of children in the looked after system, so there is a ridiculous disincentive to set up a scheme like this.
>
> (Senior Manager, Authority B)

Recording children receiving support care as looked after children had a particular impact on LAC statistics when – as had been the case in at least one authority until recently – each session of support care was counted as a separate episode of care, rather than the whole series of placements being counted as one episode.

Recruitment barriers

Finding people prepared to offer short-break fostering had not proved a barrier to developing schemes, nor did it appear to have led to competition with mainstream fostering for a limited pool of carers, as some survey respondents had feared. The main reason was that recruitment for support care targeted different groups who would mostly not have been in a position to foster full time, such as individuals in full-time employment who wanted to foster but had felt they could not do so because they worked. Indeed, in one authority, in-house recruitment had led to several child and family social workers offering support care at evenings or weekends.

Rather than deflecting potential carers from mainstream fostering, it appeared that support care could offer a way in to full-time fostering when the carer's circumstances changed. Schemes were described as a way for people to 'dip a toe in the water', and engage in some caring work even if they did not currently have adequate accommodation or enough emotional space in the family for fostering full time. Support care could also prevent mainstream foster carers from leaving the service entirely. In five local authorities running schemes, former foster carers who had decided to retire (through age, health-related problems or general disillusionment) had moved across to support fostering. This indicates that authorities may be able to retain individuals with well-developed skills – who would otherwise be lost to the service – by offering them a different (and perhaps more varied) role.

Local authorities were asked about potential recruitment strategies and particular groups whom they thought would have skills suited to support care work. Co-ordinators in authorities with schemes, and managers in those without, identified very similar groups to target as support carers. Childminders were particularly noted as having skills and training which could be extended into support care work, although two co-ordinators reported that they would have concerns over 'poaching' childminders for the service (the potential for childminders to provide support care is explored further in Chapter 7). Two authorities with schemes noted that a high percentage of their support carers were the adult children of foster carers who had grown up with a clear and realistic awareness of the realities of fostering. Such carers may in the future make the transition into full-time fostering when it fits in with their other domestic and employment responsibilities. Nurses (in an area which had experienced several hospital closures), childcare, residential home, teaching and social work staff were also noted as potential carers who may be willing to combine employment with caring.

Interviewees were also keen to draw in new carers from among the general public, rather than simply targeting professionals or those with prior experience of caring work. Specialist recruitment campaigns were noted as potential ways of overcoming barriers to recruitment, as well as sending information on support care to individuals who enquired about mainstream fostering, but who were not considered suitable for such a role (for example, on health, age, or employment grounds).

Finally, 'word of mouth' recruitment was mentioned by a number of interviewees, with both staff and carers providing examples of relatives and friends who had become carers after hearing about the possibility of part-time fostering. Indeed, in one local authority, after the first same-sex couple became support carers an increasing number of enquiries were received from within the gay community, allowing access to a wider pool of potential carers.

While one manager (in an authority without a scheme) anticipated that it might prove more difficult to find support carers willing to take placements other than at weekends, recruitment issues did not appear to operate as a major barrier to the development of support care schemes overall. On the contrary, it appeared that the development of projects could lead to the increased availability of mainstream placements, as individual carers move between different forms of fostering.

> I think it encourages the service [as a whole] really ... if we hadn't been able to take them on a part-time basis, these people would have been turned away.
>
> (Co-ordinator, Authority E)

Financial and resource barriers

Resource issues (staffing, payment and funding) were noted as a significant barrier to the development of support foster care schemes by local authorities responding to our screening survey, and also featured strongly in the interviews. Authorities with schemes had often struggled to develop them due to funding constraints, and authorities without schemes thought that it would be difficult to allocate money to such preventative work. Only one authority without a scheme felt that finances could be found to support such a project, as a strong commitment existed within this authority to developing preventative services. All other interviewees without support care schemes noted that within their authorities, current priorities tended to focus on managing placements of children who were in the looked after system, with preventative initiatives representing a far lower priority, although managers recognised the potential value of being able to offer support care. One manager noted that the department had hoped to develop a support fostering service, but had been unsuccessful in bidding for funding, while others referred to the need to support children in mainstream or kinship care placements as a higher priority:

> We're struggling to release money into family support because it is all tied up in hugely high cost placements. [We] hope to redirect towards family support, but it takes time.
>
> Manager, Authority K

> Preventative work has taken a bit of a hammering. The focus is on areas with performance indicators, and it's difficult to demonstrate that preventative work reduces the number of looked after children.
>
> Manager, Authority J

Even within authorities that had set up (or were in the process of setting up) support care schemes, only two co-ordinators reported that they had always been financially well supported by their authorities. Again, much depended on the strategic priorities of the local authority and the extent of support from senior managers for preventative work. Support care schemes were vulnerable to funding cuts unless they were clearly integrated into an overall strategy of providing a range of services to support families. The experience of a number of schemes that had 'fallen off the edge' when local authorities reorganised services, or when a particularly supportive manager left their post, attested to the importance of support care being a recognised part of the authority's service provision, rather than what one co-ordinator described as 'a sort of tacked-on offshoot'. It was noticeable that, in projects which had been incorporated into the authority's strategic plans for children's services (four projects in total, two in the previous year), management support for – and departmental recognition of – support care had increased. Carers were paid more or less in line with mainstream foster carers; and capacity existed for development work. One co-ordinator described the difference that being 'mainstreamed' in this way had made:

> [In the past] I've felt as if I've been backed by one person at a time and if something happens and they're not there any more then I have felt adrift. It hasn't been properly provisioned as part of mainstream. I haven't quite known where I belong and who's going to be backing me and what's going to happen next year ... I've been living in that kind of atmosphere for most of the time of the scheme really ... It does feel different now, I feel establishment now.
>
> Co-ordinator, Authority A

Inevitably the low priority placed on support care schemes had had an impact on the work-loads of co-ordinators. Four interviewees described their attempts to balance the demands of arranging placements, recruiting and supporting carers (sometimes in evenings and weekends), organising training, and in some cases also carrying out their own administrative tasks. In three of these cases, the co-ordinators had all worked on the projects on a part-time basis prior to accessing additional funding. While co-ordinators all demonstrated a remark-able degree of attachment and commitment to operating schemes, the stress of working under such conditions had clearly represented a heavy workload. Five co-ordinators reported tensions at times with colleagues in children and families teams, who could sometimes misunderstand the nature of the support care service; consider it to be low priority; fail to attend reviews or support children once they had been placed; or place the co-ordinator under pressure to use support carers for inappropriate placements, such as when children required full-time care in an emergency.

> I think the difficulties come because of the pressures on resources and as much as I will try to keep [emergency placements] out of our system ... at the end of the day we know there isn't another bed for that child and that is what causes the problems and once [we've got them] we can't get them moved on, and then the very tense conversations start.
>
> Co-ordinator, Authority C

Skills needed to provide support care

Five survey respondents noted that lack of relevant skills might prove a barrier to provision of support care in their authorities. A particular skill needed by support carers is the ability to work with parents as well as children. In practice, seven out of eight co-ordinators with schemes (one authority had not yet made any placements) noted that the relationship between parents and carers had not proved problematic, and that in general parents greatly welcomed the input and support offered by carers. The role of the support carer was generally restricted to signposting, befriending, providing advice to and listening to parents, rather than more direct work (which in some cases was undertaken by a family resource or family support worker while the support carer worked with the child).

While carers could on occasion feel over-burdened by parents' demands (see Chapter 6), most were mature, experienced, pragmatic individuals who were able to establish clear boundaries. Typical comments included:

> I don't really take it on board, I listen a bit, but you can't just keep taking it on board.

> You've got to be quite firm. You've got to draw your own boundaries with the parents. Get as involved as you want to get involved, not as involved as they want you involved.

Carers in general appeared unconcerned about accessing training to work with parents, and considered that their own experiences and common sense enabled them to deal with parents in an appropriate manner. In several cases, fostering training tailored for support carers did include a session on working with parents, but in the main, carers' level of engagement with parents depended upon their own individual personalities and preference for ways of working. Given that support carers in all authorities within this study underwent training as foster carers, and that scheme co-ordinators were generally very satisfied with the interpersonal skills and professionalism of their carers, it did not appear that difficulty in recruiting people with appropriate skills was a meaningful barrier to the development of support care schemes. If necessary, training programmes could be adapted to include additional sessions on working with parents, perhaps to replace elements of the mainstream fostering training which are less appropriate for support carers.

Organisational issues

The concerns expressed by some scheme managers about the appropriate location for support care services, and the inadvisability of too close an identification with family placement services, have already been discussed in Chapter 3. Five of the six managers without schemes who were interviewed for this study also identified concerns over 'ownership of the scheme' as a major barrier to development of support fostering projects. They felt that support care should either be placed under the auspices of family support, or in some halfway house between family support and fostering.

> [It] would be needed by family support, but would be run by the looked after children section.
>
> Manager, Authority J

> One of the issues we would have, is where that service is managed – is it within the family placement service, or in the family support service? I think that there are good arguments for it being managed in the family support service.
>
> Manager, Authority L

A particular problem was that links were often poor between different teams within social services – for example, between family support or area child and family teams on the one hand, and family placement/fostering and adoption services on the other. It was apparent when we explored the role of childminders as potential providers of support care (see Chapter 7) that child and family teams in most authorities used childminders to provide daytime care for children in need, financed from family support (s17) budgets. Yet there appeared to be little co-ordination of this form of support with the often similar service provided by support care schemes, using foster carers and fostering budgets and requiring children to be treated as 'looked after' if they remained with the carer overnight.

Several interviewees indicated that the lack of communication between departments would present a barrier to developing support care as part of a range of options that could be offered to families. For example, the fostering service manager in one authority (without a support care scheme) noted that there was limited overlap between his department and the assessment and family support teams. He remarked that 'bridges would need to be built' if they were to develop such a scheme, as this would be seen 'more as sitting in the family support camp' (Authority P). Such barriers are not insurmountable. Authority C, for example, was attempting to develop a 'seamless service', and the manager of the support care scheme also managed the emergency duty team and a short-stay residential children's home. To illustrate the way that support care could be offered as part of a flexible response, she gave an example of a situation that had occurred the night before the interview.

> The family broke down and the police brought the children to the area duty office. A member of staff immediately went out to the [family] home, managed to get the children home. There were obviously some problems but it was not an active case. They did a very brief initial assessment last night, referred it to the team today and we are going to jump in straight away with some short breaks and other support packages.

In this authority, close links had been developed between the family support teams, short-break scheme and family placement workers. The monies for the support care project were ringfenced within the fostering budget, and a separate s17 budget existed to support placements within the scheme. In this way, financial responsibility for (and awareness of) the scheme appeared to cross team boundaries, allowing a sense of ownership of the project across several departments, and potentially limiting internal resource competition.

Discussion

Contrary to the expectations of survey participants, barriers to development of support foster care schemes appeared to be less recruitment- and service user-based than organisational and resource-driven. The experiences of staff in authorities with schemes, and the identification exercise carried out by senior managers in areas which do not at present offer support care, broadly coincide in recognising the existence of a largely untapped workforce who could be recruited to undertake support care if structures (and political will) were in place to facilitate the development of such schemes. While clear barriers to developing support care (staff resources, funding, departmental structures) do exist, these could be overcome by refocusing a local authority's attention towards the development of innovative ways of supporting families, possibly through exploring new sources of partnership funding.

5 Costs and outcomes

Support care provides parents with short-term focused support which aims to help keep families together. If it is able to prevent children becoming accommodated on a longer-term basis, it is likely to be a cost-effective service and avoid potential trauma for both children and their families. This study sought information on the cost of establishing and running a support care service, as well as any evidence that councils were able to provide regarding the outcomes for children and families receiving such support.

Costs of support care schemes

Sources of funding

Five of the six established support care schemes were financed through fostering service budgets. The sixth had originally been developed from a sponsored childminding scheme, but had expanded with joint funding from social services (through Choice Protects) and the health authority (through the Sure Start programme). Grants provided through Choice Protects had had a significant impact, both in allowing existing schemes to expand and new ones to develop. Of the eight schemes considered in this chapter, six had received funding through the initiative. Four of these grants had since ended, but the value of the projects had been recognised and they were now being funded through mainstream fostering budgets.

The appropriate source of funding for support care schemes was raised as an issue by several managers in authorities that did not have a scheme. They suggested that such schemes might be more appropriately located – and financed – through child and family (or family support) team budgets. For example, the fostering service manager in one authority, who was developing a scheme to provide respite placements for other foster carers, noted that when the scheme was extended to support families it would probably be necessary to approach children's services about funding for this aspect of the work.

None of the schemes required parents to contribute to the cost of support care, although in one area some form of means testing was shortly to be introduced for those (few) families with working parents, in line with charges levied for respite care for disabled children.

Payments to carers

Deciding on an appropriate level of fees for providing support care had been difficult for a number of schemes. One co-ordinator described concerns within the fostering unit when the scheme was first being developed:

> How to pay support carers a reward for the job that's going to make it meaningful for them but at the same time not put it too high … the fear was [that] the people who

were doing it long term would defect in droves and want to become support carers ... so you had to kind of pitch the fees so that it doesn't attract people away from the long-term job.

Co-ordinator, Authority A

In fact, this co-ordinator felt that such fears were not justified and that people tended to be interested in providing one kind of care or the other, according to their interests and circumstances.

Generally, payment for support care was very low considering the demanding nature of the work. The Fostering Network's recommended minimum allowances (in 2003) for full-time care were between £103 per week (for someone caring for a baby) and £187 per week (for providing foster care to a young person over 16), although in practice more than half of councils have been shown to pay less than this (Hayes 2003). It is difficult to make direct comparisons between those providing short-break and full-time care, as many of those we interviewed pointed out. The families served may have differing levels of need, and the amount of care provided is very different. Support carers commonly provide care for only one or two weekends a month, whereas even respite foster carers, who work part time, frequently offer full-time care over short periods, such as when the main carer is on holiday.

The support care schemes in our study varied in their approach to the level of pay or allowances that carers could receive. Four of the six established schemes based their allowances for support carers on the rate for mainstream foster carers, although in one case allowances were based on the lowest mainstream carers' level. Two schemes also paid a retainer fee to recognise the intermittent nature of the work (in one case approximately £150 per month, which was also expected to cover initial meetings with families before a placement was agreed; and in the other, the equivalent of two nights' care per month). The third authority offered a £30 'weekend recreational allowance' as part of the support care scheme, which was not available to mainstream foster carers, so that children could be taken on outings and to leisure facilities.

The remaining two schemes paid a sessional fee for blocks of time when children were cared for. For example, one authority divided the day into four blocks (morning, afternoon, evening and overnight) and paid £8 for a weekday session and slightly more for a session at weekends. A carer looking after a child for ten sessions a week – for example, Monday to Friday 9.00 am to 3.00 pm – would thus receive £80, which was less than the average for private childminding in that area. If a child was cared for on a full-time basis in this scheme (including overnight) for one week, the payment would theoretically work out at substantially more than that received by full-time foster carers, but such full-time care rarely happened. In the other authority, however, support carers were often asked to take 'emergency' placements on a full-time basis, which earned them over £200 per week when paid at the sessional rate for support care. This caused some resentment among full-time foster carers, who received less.

The two schemes under development had so far focused on providing respite care to enable full-time foster carers to have a break. One of these schemes based payments to support carers on the scale used by the Link scheme, which provides short breaks for disabled children. This was similar to Level 3 foster care payments at £18 for a 12-hour session. The support/respite carers also received a 'boarding out' fee and clothing and holiday allowances, all paid on a pro rata basis. Carers in this scheme could provide a maximum of 28 sessions (14 full days) a month, which allowed them to cover periods when a child's main foster carer went on holiday. The other developing scheme also used support carers to provide respite for mainstream foster carers rather than families, and used a tiered payment system depending on skill levels, as for mainstream carers, with a retainer fee to cover periods when a child was not placed.

Overall costs

In general, based upon the limited data interviewees were able to supply on the costs of schemes, support care appears to be significantly less costly than providing care for accommodated children once initial start-up costs have been taken into account. One co-ordinator noted that 'to place a child in support care for a weekend once a month for a year would cost the same as one week in an external placement'. The direct costs (retainers and fees) of placements in this authority averaged £550 per child, although the length of individual placements varied considerably. Another co-ordinator calculated that the whole support care budget, including her salary, was less than the cost of a family of three in an out-of-county placement for a year. Several managers described support care as 'investing to save', and believed that it had to be cost-effective compared to the costs of full-time accommodation for children.

In some cases, lower costs were a result of lower payments to support carers; in others, purely because fewer sessions were provided per child or young person than if the case had reached the stage where accommodation had to be provided on either a short- or longer-term basis. Training could usually be provided from the fostering team's training budget or using in-house trainers and so did not add to the overall costs of setting up a scheme.

Two of the case study authorities were able to provide more detailed figures for the cost of their support care service. Both schemes had been set up and had operated for a number of years on very small budgets, but had recently been allocated additional funding to enable them to continue on a more secure basis and to expand their service. The new budgets of between £200,000 to £250,000 covered the salary of a co-ordinator, two or 2.5 support workers, an administrative worker, fees for around 20 support carers and (in one case) a small equipment budget. One of the schemes paid a monthly allowance of around £150 to support carers, plus a top-up fee for each day or part day that a child was placed. The other paid carers at sessional rates, without a retainer. These schemes were providing short breaks for between 100 and 150 children a year, and were expecting to expand once the new funding and posts had bedded in.

Discussions with co-ordinators and managers in authorities with support care schemes highlighted the importance of sufficient funding to employ an experienced co-ordinator to oversee the project and staff to offer support to carers. Several workers in schemes recounted tales of attempting to organise support care while still having other fostering service responsibilities. The nature of support care work – which often entails evening or weekend work for staff who go out on visits, arrange meetings between carers and families, attend and arrange training and provide support during unsociable hours – suggests that a dedicated team is needed, or at least an arrangement which ensures sufficient support is available from other members of the fostering service, as happens in Authority F.

Outcomes

Monitoring and recording

There was very little evidence of systematic monitoring of support care placements, although one scheme did keep detailed records and produced an annual report. In one authority, children receiving short breaks were deliberately omitted from formal statistics on looked after children supplied to the Department of Health (although they were recorded as such internally), in order not to inflate the number of children looked after. It is difficult to evaluate the effectiveness of support care services in the absence of reliable statistics, including information on what happens to children when they leave support care.

Co-ordinators and managers identified a number of difficulties in developing monitoring systems for their schemes. Three expressed a concern that recording children in such placements as 'children looked after' would be counterproductive in terms of meeting the government's targets for reducing the number of children in the looked after system. A key issue for most schemes had been lack of administrative support and time to undertake monitoring. It was noticeable that the two schemes that had recently received fairly substantial amounts of additional funding had both been able to create administrative support posts and were developing plans for regular monitoring of support care placements and the impact of the schemes. In one case, this included considering whether there had been a reduction in the number of child protection referrals and new episodes of care in areas where the support care scheme was planning to extend its service.

Preventing children becoming accommodated

One measure of the success of support care is its ability to prevent children needing to be looked after away from their families on a longer-term basis. As discussed above, this was the basis on which most co-ordinators and managers believed that support care represented 'good value for money'. Few schemes collected systematic information on what happened to children after they had received support care, but Authority B was able to demonstrate that out of about 250 referrals to the scheme over a year, only a handful of children (seven in the most recent year) went on to be accommodated. In these cases, the co-ordinator felt that the service had usually been offered too late. In Authority D, too, very few children or young people had gone from support care into the looked after system.

In Authority F, the scheme co-ordinator had 'counted up a minimum of 15 children who would have come into care without it', based on statements made by the primary carer and a review of case files. This included kinship placements that would otherwise have broken down. More general evidence for the effectiveness of preventative support services was provided by the fact that numbers of children looked after in this authority had risen when family centres were closed, which had been one of the main justifications for developing the support care scheme.

Although it was difficult to provide 'hard' evidence, many co-ordinators believed that accommodation would have occurred if short breaks had not been provided. They gave examples of families supported by the service coping with quite severe problems in the community without breaking down; Box 2 provides another example.

> He [boy receiving regular short breaks] is quite a difficult lad, and, well, you know what happens in the system, they get one placement breakdown after another and then that awful spiral and he would probably have ended up in a very expensive so-called therapeutic unit. But it's working as it is.
>
> Co-ordinator, Authority C

Box 2: Support for kinship care

A teenage boy placed with his aunt, who had three children of her own, had been excluded from school. The support carer collected him from his aunt's house in the morning and took him back at the end of the afternoon, on four days a week. The carer said: 'If I didn't, he would get to her so much she would say I can't foster this child any more.'

Further evidence for the effectiveness of support care in preventing accommodation was put forward by a co-ordinator who had noticed that when the authority had been unable to meet a request for support care – either because the situation involved chronic need (the service was targeted at families experiencing a short-term crisis), or because the scheme was simply unable to meet demand – there had often been a deterioration in the family's circumstances, resulting in the child ending up in full-time foster care.

> If we weren't able to make a placement we look at it at our placement meeting every week, and in quite a few cases we've found some months later that we're looking at accommodation. The parents simply haven't been able to cope.
>
> Co-ordinator, Authority F

The existence of a support care scheme could also affect outcomes for children by influencing social workers' approach to families in difficulties. In Authority A, where the scheme operated in one part of the city but not others, a senior manager noted that social workers appeared less likely to 'rush into full accommodation ... there is a different mindset in teams which have that understanding and access to the neighbourhood care scheme'.

Carers who took part in the three focus groups were also able to provide many examples of situations where they could see the service had made a real difference to families, giving children stability and security and giving parents a chance to sort out their problems.

> I've had parents who've come back to me and said without the service they would have cracked up and put the children into accommodation, or gone under.
>
> Support carer, Focus group A

Co-ordinators reported that parents generally valued the service highly. Several schemes asked parents to complete an evaluation form when the support care ended, and although response rates were often low, the forms that were completed showed that parents were generally very satisfied with the service and felt involved in and consulted about the support they and their children received.

Promoting continuity and stability for children

It is worth noting that keeping children out of care is not the only measure of a successful outcome for children receiving support care; short breaks can also provide continuity and stability for children when used alongside periods of accommodation (see Box 3). In another case, a support carer was able to help a young woman to build a better relationship with her stepmother, both while the girl was living at home and when she eventually returned to the care system. This improved relationship meant that the young woman was better supported by her family, even though she was no longer living at home. Support care could also be used as part of a plan to return children home to parents under a supervision order, and enable them to rejoin their families earlier than might otherwise have been the case.

> [Before the scheme] I think social workers might have been very cautious, and the child would have remained looked after by full-time carers.
>
> Co-ordinator, Authority C

In several authorities, support carers were registered for short-term mainstream fostering as well as short breaks, so that in an emergency a child who had accessed support care could be accommodated with a carer they had already come to know. Three carers who participated in focus groups noted that they had been (and in one case still was) a long-term mainstream carer of a child for whom they had initially provided support care. In each of these cases, when the child needed to be accommodated the carer was approached to offer a short-term mainstream placement, and subsequently was approved as a long-term carer for that child. While neither co-ordinators or carers particularly welcomed the idea of

---

Box 3: Flexible support

Two young children whose mother has quite severe mental health problems are provided with short breaks on a regular basis by a support carer in Authority E. When their mother is admitted to hospital, the carer looks after them full time, so they know where they will be going and it offers them continuity of care. The authority is committed to continuing this arrangement for as long as it is needed.

The scheme manager described how much the placement meant to the children. 'They hadn't been able to talk to their social worker about it, about their fears and loyalty to their mother, but because they know this carer very well, and know that they will go back and see her again when their mother is ill, they are actually able to talk to her quite a lot about it. At the review, the little boy said, "I can talk about my mummy and she hugs me," and it was lovely knowing that those children got that support.'

---

support care placements developing in this manner, it was acknowledged that in such circumstances, the fact that support carers could offer such continuity provided the greatest stability for a child.

The evidence obtained in this study strongly suggests that providing short breaks for children in need enables them to remain with their families, and may avoid longer-term care. The service is valued by parents, and it can be used in a variety of ways (including alongside accommodation) to promote continuity and stability for children. However – as many of those interviewed were themselves aware – it is difficult, on the basis of the available evidence, to demonstrate that accommodation would have occurred even if short breaks had not been provided. There is a need for schemes to collect better information about the users of their service and what happens to them, and for well-designed research studies to be carried out comparing outcomes for children receiving support care with children in similar circumstances who do not receive such help. There is also a need for better information about the costs of operating schemes. This information was often not available, especially when support care was financed through the general fostering budget.

6 The motivation and experience of support carers

Providing short breaks for children in need and supporting their parents requires particular qualities in potential carers. Support care scheme co-ordinators referred to the value of carers' life-experience in building empathy with families and awareness of the practical and emotional problems faced by parents:

> My view is that people who have struggled with quite a lot of difficulties in their lives actually make better carers than people who sail through with few problems, because they understand a lot.
>
> Co-ordinator, Authority B

> There is a type of person who just seems to be more successful ... very easy going, rough and ready household, you know, where nothing fazes them.
>
> Co-ordinator, Authority A

The task of providing support care was viewed as significantly different from the role of mainstream foster carers. One co-ordinator described it as 'substituting for a missing grandparent or auntie or friend, not substituting for a parent ... it's a different kind of role, about making parents feel empowered and not that somebody else is taking over'.

This section of the report presents the findings from three focus groups held in case study areas, involving a total of 20 carers. The carers provided information on their background, routes into caring, experience of providing support care and areas of concern which they wanted to see addressed.

Background of carers

All but two carers (a Black British married couple) who participated in focus groups were of White British origin. Many had grown-up or teenage children. As a group, the carers in the focus groups were, broadly speaking, working class and lived in similar communities to those where they were providing care, although in other authorities we were told that support carers came from a variety of backgrounds and included professionals such as teachers, social workers and doctors.

The great majority of carers in the focus groups were employed or self-employed, often working in caring professions or the public sector as care assistants, mainstream respite foster carers, childminders or teaching assistants. A few operated small businesses such as mobile hairdressing or teaching sports at community and after-school centres. One carer (a lone parent) was in receipt of income support, which significantly limited her ability to receive payments for support care. In this particular case, the erratic nature of the service (some weekends with placements, others without) meant that the carer was more financially secure receiving benefits and a small earnings disallowance than attempting to claim Working Family Tax Credit, although she would have preferred to work for a salaried service which would enable her to increase her earnings. Two other carers noted that they had taken early retirement and thus received employment pensions to supplement their earnings from support care.

The 20 carers who participated in the focus groups consisted of three married couples and one half of another dual registered partnership (the husband remained at home to care for the child placed with them); seven married women whose husbands were not registered as carers, but who inevitably were involved in support care when children were in place-ment; and six 'lone carers', including one lone male carer who had been half of a fostering partnership prior to his divorce. Three of the lone parents had adolescent children living at home. All but three carers (one married couple and one single female) had raised children of their own, and apart from the lone parents, only three interviewees still had young adult children living at home, usually in their late teens and early 20s. Several carers mentioned having grandchildren, and in four cases, explicitly referred to arranging to see grand-children when they did not have children placed with them.

Routes into caring

Six carers had been mainstream foster carers who had decided to leave the service, or limit the placements they accepted. In one example, an emergency foster parent had handed in her notice after a particularly difficult placement, during which she received no support from the children's social worker. Shortly afterwards she was contacted by the support care scheme co-ordinator. 'She said would I be interested [in offering support care] and I was, and I love it.' A further eight interviewees (including two sets of jointly registered spouses) had been childminders before joining Authority A's support care scheme. The remaining six carers (including one couple) had been newly recruited to support care from a range of backgrounds. These new recruits had either contemplated fostering for some years but believed they were ineligible, or had relatives and friends who were carers and who had introduced them to the concept of 'part-time fostering'.

Motivation for undertaking support care

There was little difference in motivation for undertaking support care work between the childminders, those who were fulfilling long-held ambitions to foster, and those who already possessed extensive knowledge of fostering but no longer wished to continue providing full-time care. Regardless of routes into support care, all participants in the focus groups stressed the satisfaction of providing children with stability and access to a 'normal' life.

> It's giving them a break, pick them up from school, get them down the park, have a picnic, the normal stuff ... sometimes you go to bed with a throbbing headache, think-ing I can't wait for tomorrow to come, but for every day like that, there's a week or a month of fun, of knowing that you are doing something worthwhile and getting paid for it.

> It's about giving them a normal life, a lot of the children might not have any idea ...

They also described the improvement to adult lives which could be made by carers, citing examples where support care had eased the stress on parents and enabled them to cope, sometimes to enter training or employment, and to generally 'get themselves together'. Although carers tended to focus on the needs of children over and above that of parents, a clear consensus of opinion existed that by assisting both parents and children to modify certain behaviours and responses, they could improve the situation for families under extreme stress. They shared their strategies for dealing with difficult behaviour with parents without undermining their confidence:

> I find that parents, who are probably caring parents but they haven't got parenting skills, the way they do things has made the children very often the way they are, but you can't tell parents that because they aren't bad people you know, but you do find they respond to the positive [examples].

The support carers were clearly proud of the service they provided, and the generally positive outcomes for families.

> I think it's really rewarding. It really is. I get a lot out of it personally. Just to think you're, you know, improving their life and giving them a bit of care they wouldn't get at home.

The changing face of service users

Carers in all three focus groups reported that over the time they had been providing the service, a change had occurred in the type of work they were expected to undertake. While carers had initially been recruited to provide respite for parents and children, to offer some form of support to parents and to provide care for 'normal' children whose families were under stress, they had increasingly found themselves dealing with children with more challenging behaviours such as autistic spectrum disorders and Attention Deficit Hyperactivity Disorder (ADHD). At times they questioned whether they were a 'last resort' for children who could not be placed elsewhere, or whose parents were contemplating accommodation due to children's behavioural problems.

> A lot of the children we have now, they've got autism and that, not just young children who need a break, it's usually now like autism and ADHD and Asperger's. In the beginning it might be perhaps a mum had gone into hospital and she'd got no back-up or someone had a new baby and had to get used to it, and then it became more domestic violence, perhaps to get the children out of that while the parents got sorted, but now …

Carers were clearly not happy about the change in their role, although none reported that they were contemplating leaving the service as a result of the shift towards working with more challenging children. One message that did come across clearly, however, was frustration that when social workers referred children to the scheme, often neither the co-ordinator nor the carer was adequately advised about the child's level of disturbance.

Impact on carer's family

Although co-ordinators felt that carers had some level of control over refusing or ending placements, carers reported that they found it difficult to refuse to take on a child once the paperwork had been prepared and an initial meeting had been carried out, or to ask for a placement to end early.

> I thought she was beyond our help, we couldn't give her any more help but I found it really hard to stop her coming … [social workers] didn't want me to [end the placement].

Several carers with children living at home (or grandchildren who came to visit) reported the impact on their families of having increasingly disturbed children in placement, with experiences of broken computers, finding young people smoking in bedrooms, 'smashed up' rooms and needing to lock their own children's rooms and toys away. Two carers reported that their older teenage children were starting to spend placement weekends away, staying at friends' or relatives' homes (although this was often regarded as a bonus by the carer's teenagers, rather than a problem). Several grandparents reported that their adult children had to rearrange visits to ensure that grandchildren were not present at the same time as support care children.

In contrast, three carers reported that not only had their grown-up children assisted with placements while they lived at home, but that some or all of their children were either engaged in caring work themselves or would 'help out' at weekends.

Overwhelmingly, carers reported that they felt the role of their own families in the provision of care was under-rated and forgotten, and that far more recognition was needed of the sacrifices made and support given by children growing up with parents who are foster carers.

Payment for support care

In two out of three case study areas the carers' biggest complaint related to low pay. Lack of funding for support care schemes had often resulted in low fees, which had not increased for many years. In all three case study areas, payment for support care was now on a par with (and in one location higher than) the lowest pay band for mainstream foster carers. However, the issues of payment for skills, access to 'activities money' and recognition of the support offered to parents remained a source of some bitterness to carers. Only one of the authorities in this study (not a case study area) made a specific payment for activities undertaken with children in placement. In all other locations, carers were expected to pay for any outings out of the placement fee.

> There's one social worker, and he actually said he wanted this weekend to be activities based, and I said, 'Look, I don't have the money to do this, if you want activities you have to pay for them, or you have to ask the child's parents …' and he said, 'Well, I thought you got the money for it.'

> Don't forget if you're taking a child in your care out to the pictures, you've also got to take your own, you've also got to take yourself, and that's to come out of your £20 a day or whatever.

The practice of either making use of a specific (lower) pay scale for support carers, or locating them within the lowest level of the fostering pay range, caused particular resentment given the level of support offered to parents and the complex needs of some children in placement. One carer made the point that part-time placements were very different to full-time foster care:

> The big difference is that the time that you have children in support care is much shorter than the 24 hours a day that you have them in foster care, but it's much more intense. You have to devote yourself entirely to the children for the time you've got them, whereas in a foster care situation they just become part of the family.

Support carers who had been former mainstream foster carers were particularly critical of pay levels, as they usually received a pay cut on moving to support care, regardless of their years of experience or level of skills. Delays in receipt of support care payments were also cited as a major problem, with carers in all three authorities recounting considerable difficulties caused by bureaucratic delays and complicated payment systems. In one authority (as confirmed by the co-ordinator), fees were sometimes received up to eight weeks in arrears, or paid at the wrong rate of pay, and in another authority, carers had not received a promised backdated pay increase several months after the date when it should have commenced.

Overall, carers indicated that even if their pay scale could not be increased, they felt allowances for activities with children should be available, account should be taken of additional time spent working with parents (even if only on a nominal basis), and clear guidelines should be provided to cover carers' entitlement to receipt of allowances for equipment and clothing. The study highlighted the need for greater communication between mainstream fostering services and support care teams, and the importance of well-developed financial procedures and policies covering all forms of placement made with support carers.

Support from the local authority

The level of support offered to foster carers can be as important as the level of financial reward in encouraging them to enter and continue in the work (Social Services Inspectorate 2002). The carers who participated in the focus groups had mixed feelings about their relationship with the local authority and the extent to which they felt the service they provided was valued by those outside the scheme. They often felt that they were unable to access adequate information on children before accepting a placement, and could also find themselves pressurised to continue caring for a child when they felt that the placement was unsuitable. While acknowledging that some social work staff were effective and thorough, others were perceived to be dismissive of carers, unaware of the limitations of the service, or simply disinterested in the child and carer. However, carers in all focus groups repeatedly stressed how much they valued the support of scheme co-ordinators and support workers. Although they often went on to express dissatisfaction with the way support care workers were treated, they stressed that this was a result of wider social services policies and relationships with particular social workers, rather than difficulties with the support care scheme itself.

Minor concerns about relationships with support care staff related to lack of clarity over access to training and inflexibility over altering placement dates. In two authorities, carers referred to initiatives which would have benefited them, such as the authority providing foster carers with a home computer for the use of children placed with them, but which turned out not to be available to support carers. Incidents like these resulted in them feeling sidelined and forgotten in comparison with mainstream carers. Those carers who had worked in mainstream foster care were generally more alert to these discrepancies than individuals who had worked exclusively in support care.

Another issue of concern raised by some carers was their difficulty in finding out about ongoing training, although they were theoretically entitled to attend the same sessions as mainstream foster carers.

> We've had a form asking me what training I've done, but I've never had a form saying, right, 'this is available, that's available'.

Even where carers were kept apprised of training events, the fact that support carers were almost all in paid employment meant that attendance at sessions could be extremely difficult, as most courses were run during the week in working hours. In two authorities, carers noted that as they were paid on a sessional basis for support care, they had to lose money to attend a training course, because it meant either cancelling a booked placement or taking time off from other employment. Carers were not paid to attend training sessions, despite the fact that ongoing skills updates were often a requirement of their registration as a foster carer.

Support groups for carers were generally infrequent, despite the best intentions of co-ordinators. The fact that these groups had to take place during evenings or weekends (requiring overtime for paid staff, and access to council buildings out of hours) meant that support carers rarely met up as a group. When they did (as when they participated in the focus groups), the sharing of experiences was found to be very helpful.

One other area of concern, mentioned by scheme co-ordinators as well as carers, was the pressure placed on carers to accept emergency placements of children. While the majority of carers felt that it was clearly in the best interests of children who had been receiving support care to return to a carer they already knew in an emergency situation, several focus group participants reported that they had also experienced considerable pressure to accept emergency placements of children they did not know, on the grounds that they were registered for such situations. In some cases, carers had found themselves looking after children for several months at a time, when they initially understood that a child would remain with them for a few days or a fortnight.

We found that support carers were very committed to the service they offered, and prepared to spend considerable amounts of their own time ensuring that the children placed with them had a positive experience. In one authority, the support carers had engaged in fundraising activities to purchase a holiday caravan where they could take children receiving support care. However, the conditions under which they worked – and the increasing pressure to accept more challenging children – were leading in some cases to cynicism towards social services departments and dissatisfaction with the way in which they felt their service was marginalised from mainstream structures. The support of scheme co-ordinators, and the buffer they provided in their dealings with the wider social services department, helped to explain why many carers had remained with the service so long.

7 Childminders and support care

Introduction

This chapter considers the potential for support care services to build on the childcare service already provided by registered childminders. Until 2001, the regulation of childcare services (including childminding) was undertaken by under-eights officers or inspectors at a local authority level, with considerable variation in the standards that were applied. In September 2001, the transfer of responsibility for registration and inspection to the Office for Standards in Education (Ofsted) led to the development of national standards for childcare (DfES 2001).

The guidance on standards for childminders includes an appendix setting out additional criteria to be met by childminders who wish to care for children overnight, for a continuous period of not more than 27 days (after this, the guidance notes that they should be regarded as a foster child and the carer must notify the social services department). A new category of childminder registered to work in the child's own home, called a home childcarer, was also created in April 2003. These new developments make it possible for childminders to offer a similar service to the support care schemes that have been developed within fostering services, without needing to be approved as foster carers when children stay overnight. However, before this study was carried out, little was known about the impact of these regulatory changes or the extent to which childminders were offering such placements.

Information to address this question was obtained from a number of sources. First, we re-contacted the co-ordinators of six community childminding schemes (providing places for children in need) who had participated in an earlier TCRU study of sponsored day care in 1997/8. In telephone interviews, they were asked about the impact of changes in the regulation of childminding and home childcare, and whether community childminding schemes had the potential to expand into support care work and an interest in doing so. Secondly, a short questionnaire was included in a newsletter sent by the National Childminding Association to co-ordinators of childminding networks across England in July 2003. The questionnaire asked about the number of childminders registered to provide overnight care; whether any offered short breaks for children in need; if this was a service the network would want to develop, and whether there were particular difficulties that would need to be overcome before childminders could offer such a service. Finally, the interviews with fostering service managers and support care scheme co-ordinators included a question about the use of childminders for this work, and any advantages or difficulties this might create.

Community childminding schemes revisited

None of the six community childminding schemes involved in the earlier TCRU study were actively developing a short-break or overnight care service. The main barrier perceived by co-ordinators was the unwillingness of most childminders to work evenings or weekends because of the impact on their own family lives. This mirrors the findings of other studies examining the views and motivations of childcare providers (Statham and Mooney 2003; Mooney *et al.* 2001). However, in most schemes co-ordinators were aware of one or two childminders who did provide overnight care for children placed by social services, but on an occasional and informal basis rather than being specifically registered to do so. In most of these situations, the child was already being cared for by the childminder during the day, and staying overnight with the same carer provided continuity in circumstances such as the mother going into hospital, or a grandparent carer needing a break. Some childminders were foster carers or had been in the past, but this was not a requirement for providing overnight care. However, childminders taking children placed by social services would have gone through an additional assessment (beyond basic childminder registration) in order to belong to the community scheme. One authority had in the past undertaken a special assessment if children were to stay overnight, but now relied on the Ofsted regulations for providers of overnight care.

Co-ordinators also reported very little take-up of the option to register as a home carer, allowing childminders to work in the child's home rather than their own. Again, the predominant feeling was that most childminders would not want to do this, and – in the particular case of children placed by social services – that the often chaotic or difficult nature of the child's home environment would make this an inappropriate option. However, some childminders within community schemes did at times work with families in their own homes. For example, one childminder helped a young teenage mother to establish a routine with her baby. Again, this was done on an informal basis rather than through specific registration as a home child carer.

All of the community childminding schemes were located within early years services or family support teams rather than within fostering services. Links between these divisions were generally not strong. Managers of community childminding schemes often had little knowledge of the extent to which the fostering service provided short breaks for children in need, and vice versa. In one authority, however, there was a greater degree of co-operation and exchange, with the fostering team calling on the childminding scheme for help when they were unable to find a placement, especially for a young child. In this example, childminders were granted temporary status as foster carers to enable them to provide these full-time placements.

Childminding networks

The introduction of the National Childcare Strategy in 1997 has led to a growth in the organisation of childminding networks, which bring together childminders in a locality and provide resources, support and training to ensure higher standards than could be expected from childminders operating in an isolated manner. Some networks have a particular focus, such as providing childcare for groups of employers or places for children in need. A short survey circulated with the network co-ordinators' newsletter received 31 responses, from networks in both rural and urban areas. Most already offered daytime care to children placed and paid for by social services, and there was support in principle for extending this to include longer periods, but it was also felt that a number of difficulties would need to be overcome. Again, a major obstacle was thought to be the reluctance of most childminders to offer overnight or weekend care because of their own family commitments (see Table 7.1). Ten networks had no childminders registered to provide overnight care, 14 had either one or two, and only two had more than four.

Table 7.1: Barriers to childminders offering overnight/support care

Barrier	Number of network co-ordinators mentioning
Fire regulations	14
Own family commitments	10
Funding issues	9
Weak links with social services	3
Lack of training/support	3
Premises (e.g. lack of bedrooms)	2
Number of co-ordinators responding to the survey	31

A small number of childminders are nevertheless likely to be interested in this kind of work, possibly those with older children rather than a young family at home. Several network co-ordinators noted that some childminders had been keen to register for overnight care, but had experienced difficulties in doing so. The main problem, mentioned by almost half of the networks responding, was meeting the fire safety standards required by Ofsted for providers of overnight care. There appeared to be some confusion and inconsistency in the application of standards in this area, and it was noted that foster carers, who also cared for non-related children overnight, were not required to install hard-wired alarms and fire doors.

> We have four community childminders [offering places to children placed by social services] but only one offers overnight care and this is solely because she is also an approved foster carer. Two of the other childminders wanted to offer this service but were 'put off' by fire service and Ofsted regulations with regard to such requirements as additional fire doors, fire alarm etc.
>
> Network co-ordinator, metropolitan area

After the survey was completed, in September 2003, Ofsted acknowledged that some of the requirements may have exceeded those necessary to meet the national standards, and amended Standard 6.14 in the National Standards for Childminding to take account of the fact that not all registered childminders would need to have a visit from a fire safety officer (Ofsted 2003). It is hoped that this will remove one source of difficulty for childminders wishing to offer overnight care, whether to parents paying privately for childcare or to social workers looking for short breaks for children in need.

Other barriers to offering support care identified by respondents were the need for additional funding and resources to cover overnight care and to pay a retainer if child-minders were expected to keep a place open; inability to provide support or monitor placements during these times; lack of additional bed space in many childminders' homes; and the need for extra training. One respondent noted that social services' payment rates for foster care were much lower than for sponsored childminders. While the majority of co-ordinators thought that a support care service was a good idea, and were committed to developing services to meet identified needs, the difficulties that childminders would face in taking on this work were summed up as follows:

> Lack of training, support, proper equipment, 24-hour helpline and sufficient funding would make it very difficult to offer this service – although, in principle, it is a good idea.
>
> Network co-ordinator, London area

Views of social care professionals

Fostering service managers in authorities without support care schemes were asked if they thought childminders would be able to carry out this work. In general, they thought that childminders (especially experienced ones working within specialist childminding schemes) would have the right kind of skills and also the advantage of good links within their local communities. However, some concerns were expressed about the advisability of combining a support care service with caring for other children while their parents were at work. Among the authorities with schemes, one had recruited a number of former childminders as support carers, and one based the support care service (known as neighbourhood care) around a group of childminders who had dual registration as part-time foster carers so that they could keep children overnight if needed. In the latter scheme, the childminders also provided 'regular' childcare for working parents, since the fees from irregular support care work gave them insufficient income. Both the childminders and the scheme co-ordinator felt that their status as childminders was important in helping families to view the service as non-stigmatising.

> They're locally known in the area as childminders, they're very much part of the community, families don't feel threatened by them.
>
> Scheme co-ordinator, Authority A

Discussion

We aimed to assess whether childminders could form the basis of a support care service in some authorities, and if they would need to be registered as foster carers to do so. The current picture is piecemeal and confused. There is certainly a potential for childminding networks and community childminding schemes to offer short breaks, including overnight or weekends, to help children remain within their families. The experience of one council showed how this could be done (see Box 4). Such a service would be an extension of the daytime care that many already offer to children in need, and would build on ad hoc arrangements where a small number of childminders already offer overnight or weekend support to families. However, several issues would need to be resolved.

One barrier has been the Ofsted requirements for registering childminders who wish to offer overnight care, in particular the inconsistency around fire safety measures, which are not required of foster carers and appear to be deterring some childminders from offering overnight care. At the time of writing, it appears that this is being resolved. A second issue is the relationship between community childminding schemes – usually located in early years and childcare/education services – and support care schemes, usually located within fostering and adoption services. The two could complement each other; for example, with one focusing on children under eight and the other on teenagers and young adolescents, or one operating a lower threshold for access while the other took children where there was an imminent risk of accommodation. Alternatively, a community childminding scheme could be extended to provide short-break support across the age range. Current Ofsted regulations for overnight care appear to eliminate the need for childminders to also be approved as foster carers, although these regulations need to be clarified and applied in a consistent manner.

Box 4: Newcastle Community Childminding Network

In 2003, this network had 14 childminders registered to provide overnight care. They provided both short-term and longer-term (up to 28-day) placements for children referred by social services, and also accepted referrals from the emergency duty team out of office hours. Childminders were paid £3 an hour up to 6.00 pm, and a one-off fee of £15 for care between the hours of 6.00 pm and 9.00 am, unless the child needed additional care during the night in which case rates were individually negotiated. Funding came from the social services Section 17 (family support) budget, and included a small budget for items such as extra bedding if these were needed. Some of the childminders were also registered as foster carers, but this was not a requirement for providing overnight care. Parents often built up a good relationship with the childminder, and could continue to use them on a private basis after the social services placement had ended.

8 | Conclusions

This small-scale, exploratory study examined barriers to the development of support care and ways in which these might be overcome. This final chapter summarises the findings in relation to a number of key questions, and identifies factors that would facilitate the development of short-break services for children in need.

Support care: some key issues

Is support care an effective way of supporting children?

Given the lack of monitoring and recording of information on children receiving support care, and in particular the lack of 'hard' data on outcomes, it is difficult to provide conclusive evidence for the effectiveness of support care. Several schemes were planning to introduce better record keeping now that their capacity had improved with additional funding, and were hoping to undertake research into outcomes for children and families who had used the service. The evidence obtained suggested that support care services were successful and much appreciated by parents. They were able to offer a flexible service that could be tailored to the particular needs of the child and family, and many examples showed how support care had been able to provide children with continuity and stability while maintaining them in the family home. Very few children who had accessed support care went on to become accommodated on a longer-term basis. This could be because they were a different group, with less severe needs than those who became looked after. However, the criterion for accessing support care in most authorities was that the service was needed in a crisis to prevent family breakdown, suggesting they did have similar needs. This was reinforced by the consensus of opinion among the professionals interviewed, who believed that the children receiving support care were a similar population to those who were accommodated, but that they had been reached at an earlier stage.

Does support care divert people from a career in mainstream fostering?

There was no evidence that this was the case. Support carers were drawn from a pool of people who would in most cases not have been available for full-time fostering (such as those in full-time employment) or those who would not wish to take on full-time fostering at their current stage of life, such as grandparents and the young adult children of foster carers. Some support care workers later moved into mainstream fostering, providing an additional source of potential recruits.

The preponderance of former mainstream foster carers in support care suggests that some carers who are currently lost to the service may welcome the opportunity of remaining in fostering if they can be made aware of the fact that alternatives to full-time care exist. Comments from former mainstream carers indicated that after some years of providing full-time care, this group often welcomed the opportunity to change their role into one of family support.

Where should a support care scheme be based?

Although the majority of schemes are currently located within family placement teams, there are arguments for considering a base within family support services. The nature of support care is distinct from mainstream fostering (a point made by both co-ordinators and carers), and support carers and staff often felt as though they did not fit comfortably into fostering services. They reported that some families could feel stigmatised by the location of the service (as well as the need for children to become looked after), and disempowered by the project's association with fostering. Most co-ordinators had tried to address such concerns by referring to the scheme as 'family support', or avoiding the use of headed paper using terms such as fostering and adoption.

However, there were also advantages for support carers of strong links to family placement services: for example, easier access to the training and support offered to mainstream foster carers, and (where support carers were also registered to provide short-term care) the possibility of families being offered a flexible service combining short breaks with longer periods of accommodation. The key message appeared to be the importance of developing close links between family placement and family support services and ensuring that support care is presented to families in an accessible, non-stigmatising way, regardless of where the service was actually based.

Must children receiving support care be treated as 'looked after'?

Children were treated as looked after (accommodated under s20 of the Children Act) in all the support care schemes in our study. However, there was considerable confusion over whether this was necessary, and several local authority lawyers who participated in this research suggested that it might be possible under a recently issued local authority circular, LAC (2003) 13, to provide support care under s17 of the Children Act instead. There is also a lack of consistency in the fact that childminders are allowed, under Ofsted regulations, to provide overnight care without such children needing to be regarded as 'looked after', and with no requirement for the childminder to be registered as a foster carer (although some are). Additional standards, however, are applied by Ofsted to childminders wishing to offer overnight care.

In the light of this confusion over the legal status of children being cared for away from home for regular short periods, all authorities reported that they would welcome clear guidance from the Department of Health on the correct procedures. Guidance is also needed on the level of documentation required to ensure that essential information exists on children receiving this form of care and that appropriate safeguards exist. We found considerable variation across schemes with regard to requirements for reviews, medicals and care plans. Most schemes had decided to operate some form of 'slimmed down' Looking After Children (LAC) procedures, but were making such decisions in isolation. For overworked social work staff (who may in some cases fail to appreciate that they are expected to attend reviews, meetings and so on once a child is in a support care placement) the level of documentation required for support care may prove an additional barrier to appropriate use of the service. One way of overcoming this barrier, and the stigma many parents associate with full LAC procedures, would be to minimise the documentary requirements for children who remain at home with their parents, are not subject to care proceedings or child protection concerns, and merely access support care on a fortnightly or monthly basis.

Developing an effective support care service

The findings from this study suggest a number of areas that local authorities need to consider when developing support care services.

Strategic planning

Information received from authorities which have developed support care schemes on a piecemeal basis indicates that staff and carers are hampered by a lack of security, low staffing levels, the need to bid for funds on an annual basis and an inability to plan and develop the service in a coherent manner. Projects which were developed in this unstructured manner have essentially continued as a result of the commitment and determination of staff and carers, often struggling on with limited funds and resultant impacts on both staff morale and service users' access to the service. Other schemes have failed when a particular manager or co-ordinator leaves their post, or short-term funding ends. Funding through the Choice Protects initiative has been welcomed by local authorities and has had a significant impact on the development of support care in many areas. Partnerships with other agencies (such as with Health and Sure Start in Authority A) have also provided additional income to enable projects to expand. However, insecurity over the fate of schemes once short-term funding ends highlights the need for projects to be incorporated into mainstream budgets (either family support or fostering) wherever possible.

An integrated strategy, where support care has a clear role within the range of council services for children, would help to ensure that preventative services like this do not lose out when decisions are being made about resource allocation. Such a strategy would also need to take a co-ordinated view of how services offered by different agencies to support families fit together – for example, the relationship between the care offered to children in need by community (or sponsored) childminders and by short-break foster carers.

Support and training for carers

The focus group discussions highlighted the importance of offering a good support package to carers, who form the backbone of any scheme. The provision of similar support to that enjoyed by mainstream carers (such as carers' group meetings, access to equipment, 24-hour 'on-call' support and regular supervision) should be no more costly than when provided for full-time foster carers, and would help to ensure that support carers feel valued and enabled in their work. Such support could be offered by dedicated workers attached to schemes, or possibly by embedding the support carers into the fostering service so that each fostering team member has some support carers on their workload, as happened in one authority in our study. When co-ordinators were running schemes single-handed, it was generally difficult for them to provide the support and supervision that carers needed. The good relationships which scheme co-ordinators had been able to establish with their support carers were repeatedly mentioned as a crucial factor in the success of the service, and it is important that they are able to allocate sufficient time to this.

Training for support carers needs to involve a mixture of weekend and evening sessions to ensure that employed carers are able to attend without loss of earnings or having to use annual leave entitlement. While most local authorities who offer support care currently ensure their carers complete the same pre-registration training as mainstream foster carers, there are arguments in favour of offering a shortened form of training, devised on an in-house basis by support care co-ordinators and managers, and focusing on issues of particular relevance to support care such as working with parents. Two authorities in our study had created opportunities for support carers to expand their role into such areas as running support groups for parents of children with ADHD (Authority B) and acting as family group conference convenors (Authority C).

Pay and allowances

Financial reward was not the primary motivation for undertaking support care work, but issues relating to pay and allowances were a source of considerable dissatisfaction to many carers. They expressed concerns about the rate of pay, which in most cases was extremely low; inconsistencies between carers within the same scheme; late payments; the expectation that they would pay for activities for children placed with them; and lack of access to resources that were available to mainstream foster carers, such as loyalty bonuses, clothing allowances and computers. They were often left feeling that their work was not valued or adequately rewarded by the local authority. Issues such as these need to be addressed when schemes are being set up, and decisions made about whether support carers are to be paid on a fostering scale (and where on the scale they should be placed) or on a specific support care rate which reflects the parental support element of their work.

Good communication

The study suggests that clearer lines of communication need to be established between various social work teams. Social workers sometimes had unrealistic expectations of what support care schemes could offer, expecting them to act as a source of emergency placements or failing to provide adequate information about the level of a child's needs. Some carers reported that they were increasingly being asked to care for children with quite severe behavioural or psychological difficulties when they were neither trained nor equipped to deal with this.

   The issue of placements for children with ADHD/autistic spectrum disorders was a major point of discussion in all three focus groups, with carers referring to the emphasis of their caring role having changed from providing support to families under stress to providing respite for parents whose children were on the verge of accommodation because of disabilities and behavioural difficulties. While carers accepted that children receiving the service often had more complex needs than when the service was initiated, they were often dissatisfied with the lack of communication and support they received from social workers, although scheme co-ordinators performed a valuable role in acting as a buffer or bridge in these situations.

Record keeping

Few support care schemes collected systematic information about the children who were placed, including records of previous or subsequent contact with social services and outcomes for children and their families. Collecting and analysing such data would enable schemes to demonstrate the impact of their service on children and families; this needs to be considered when services are being established.

Concluding comments

This study has investigated the nature and extent of support care schemes in England, and explored the barriers that might be preventing local authorities from developing this service for children in need. It has revealed a complex picture: some local authorities have developed specialist schemes to provide short breaks for children and support for their parents, while others are offering this service on an occasional or ad hoc basis using mainstream foster carers, and some community childminding networks are exploring the potential to offer a similar service (including overnight care) but under different regulations. The legal requirements for placing children in this form of care are unclear, and local authorities would welcome clarification on the issues involved, in particular whether support care needs to be provided under s20 of the Children Act or whether it can be offered as a form of family support under s17. The study suggests that there is a need for a more integrated approach to providing this kind of support to families, both at a local authority level (locating support care firmly within a spectrum of services to children and families) and at national level (for example, greater dialogue between the regulatory bodies responsible for childminding and for foster care).

Support care schemes appear able to offer a particularly flexible response to the needs of families in times of stress, and to help children to remain cared for at home. The commitment of the scheme co-ordinators and support carers to providing this service was evident throughout the study, often in difficult circumstances and for very little financial reward. In the words of one senior manager, 'It's a small resource which goes a long way.'

References

Aldgate, J. and Bradley, M. (1999) *Supporting Families Through Short-Term Fostering.* London: The Stationery Office.

Department for Education and Skills (2001) *National Standards for Day Care and Childminding. Annex B: Overnight care.* London: DfES.

Department of Health (1991) *The Children Act 1989 Guidance and Regulations: Volume 3, Family placement.* London: HMSO.

Department of Health (2003) *Children Looked After by Local Authorities: Statistics for the year ending 31 March 2002, England.* London: DH.

Fry, E. (2003) *Support Care: The future.* Unpublished paper, Fostering Network.

Hayes, D. (2003) 'Councils could be forced to pay foster carers a minimum allowance'. *Community Care,* 6–12 February: 10.

Howard, J. (1997) *A Caring Alternative: Building a new resource for young people in need and their families.* Unpublished paper, Department of Social Services, Bradford MDC.

Howard, J. (2000) 'Support care: a new role for foster carers'. In A. Wheal (ed.), *Working With Parents.* Lyme Regis: Russell House Publishing.

Mooney, A., Knight, A., Moss, P. and Owen, C. (2001) *Who Cares? Childminding in the 1990s.* Bristol/York: The Policy Press/Joseph Rowntree Foundation.

Ofsted (2003) *Day Care: Guidance to the National Standards – revisions to certain criteria.* Available HTTP: <http://www.ofsted.gov.uk/publications/docs/3382.pdf> (accessed 25 February 2004).

Packman, J. and Hall, C. (1999) *From Care to Accommodation: Support, care and control in child care services.* London: The Stationery Office.

Social Services Inspectorate (2002) *Fostering for the Future: Inspection of foster care services.* London: SSI.

Statham, J. and Mooney, A. (2003) *Around the Clock: Childcare services at atypical times.* Bristol/York: The Policy Press/Joseph Rowntree Foundation.

Statham, J., Dillon, J. and Moss, P. (2000) *Placed and Paid For: Supporting families through sponsored day care.* London: The Stationery Office.

Tarleton, B. (2003) 'Committed to caring: family based short break carers' views of their role'. *Adoption and Fostering,* 27 (1), 36–46.

Appendix

Legal issues of relevance to the development of support foster care

Background

In the research specification for this study, possible legal barriers to the introduction of support care schemes had been highlighted for exploration. Anecdotally, it had been reported that the requirement to provide support care through s20 of the Children Act, with all of the associated Looked After Children (LAC) requirements, was dissuading local authorities from developing this service. Interviews were therefore carried out with a small sample of local authority lawyers to ascertain their opinions on a range of statutory, regulatory and practical issues of relevance to development of support care schemes.

In total we interviewed representatives of six local authorities (three with schemes, and three without) to enable us to explore the views of legal officers, or policy officers with a particular involvement in the legal arena, on a number of issues pertaining to the development and delivery of support care. Topics ranged from the most appropriate legal status for children accessing services to potential or actual legal difficulties over service delivery, and whether s20 or s17 status was more beneficial in terms of achieving performance targets and with regard to demands on staff time. In addition, we examined whether legal departments might welcome DH guidance on support care schemes and, if so, what advice would prove most helpful for those authorities who operated (or were considering setting up) a project.

In two authorities which currently offer support care, information on legal issues was provided by policy departments, as a considerable overlap exists between the two sections. Indeed, a review of delivery of support care was under way in one authority, following DH guidance on offering accommodation under s17 issued under LAC (2003) 13 and amendments within the Adoption and Children Act 2002.

Legal status of children receiving support care

Currently all three local authorities offering support care regard children accessing the service as accommodated under s20 of the Children Act and hence 'looked after'. While lawyers acknowledged that s20 offered the most appropriate (indeed until recently, the only) option under present law, a clear consensus existed that s20 requirements were not entirely appropriate for short breaks.

> I think that if someone is looking after a child for a couple of nights continuously, at that point that child ought to be in the looked after system under the current law. However it is a law which needs changing to make it simpler.
>
> Lawyer, Authority B

In total, all six legal/policy officers felt that the current legislation was (at least in part) inappropriate for operating support care schemes, with three interviewees explicitly mentioning the 'stigma' of children becoming accommodated simply to receive occasional care.

S17 Children Act

Three interviewees (one in an authority with a scheme and two without) referred to the value of the amendments to the Children Act under s116 of the Adoption and Children Act 2002, which gives local authorities the power to provide accommodation under s17. Although the Adoption and Children Act was not yet in force at the time of writing, LAC (2003) 13 would theoretically permit authorities to offer respite services without the need to accommodate children.

However, all of these interviewees noted that they would have concerns over the level of protection for children being provided with support care under this section of the Act, and would wish to see strict regulatory controls to ensure that children are adequately safeguarded.

> I think it could be provided under s17 but I would want to be seeing guidance and regulations ... which would require that when these schemes are in place there are appropriate assessments and reviews.
>
> Lawyer, Authority L

One authority was actively pursuing the possibility of offering support care under s17, and policy documents under consideration at the time of interview noted that provision of care under s17 would provide the following advantages:

> Children provided with overnight accommodation will not be stigmatised by being 'in care', families will not be stigmatised by having their children received into care, the statistics for looked after children will not be swollen by children who are having a planned short term break, social workers will not need to complete the LAC paperwork or arrange LAC reviews, children will not need to have medical examinations, parents will be in no doubt that they retain total responsibility for their children although they are staying with an approved person arranged by SSD, children will not necessarily have to be allocated cases, it will be easier for placements to be arranged following referrals from our partner agencies.
>
> Discussion document prepared by Authority A

Within this authority, it was proposed that safeguarding of children could be most appropriately guaranteed by insisting that all carers were registered as foster carers 'to ensure that they can provide accommodation under s20 of the Children Act where this intervention is more appropriate', and that Fostering Regulations and National Minimum Standards for Fostering and Childminding were applied at all times.

S20 Children Act

Two interviewees felt, for reasons of certainty, and to ensure that children were adequately safeguarded in placements, that s20 would provide the most appropriate vehicle for provision of support care. However, both lawyers wished to see a modification to local authority duties and LAC paperwork in cases of short-term breaks.

Section 20 would have to apply, but ... the regulations ought to be amended to recognise the specialist nature of these schemes so that it isn't overly bureaucratic; after all, this would still provide the basic safeguards of s20 rather than the lower safeguards of s17, which are very few.

Lawyer, Authority B

There really needs to be some clarity otherwise there will be a temptation, given human nature, if there is an opt out and a way of avoiding filling in all these numerous forms, there will be pressure to say that 'this is not a looked after child'... [therefore need to ensure that any changes include] reviewing mechanisms and some element of independent reviewing. So that is what I want to see from any guidance, that there is clarity and it isn't simply left down to individual local authority's interpretation or discretion or it could potentially be abused.

Lawyer, Authority N

'New' legal status

While noting the possibilities of providing support care under either s17 or s20 of the Children Act, two lawyers (in common with several managers and co-ordinators – see Chapter 3) recommended that a new, flexible legal status should be developed which combined s20 and s17 responsibilities, to ensure flexibility while maintaining adequate safeguards.

> I think it would be much better to have a legal responsibility which is unique to these circumstances.
>
> Lawyer, Authority C

> I don't think the current requirements under s20 or the current guidance [LAC (2003) 13] fit this scenario, we would need to look at something which is newly devised.
>
> Lawyer, Authority L

Precedents for amendment/provision of support care

As noted above, three lawyers cited amendments to s17 of the Children Act 1989 enacted by s116 of the Adoption and Children Act 2003, and the DH Circular LAC (2003) 13 as appropriate ways of avoiding the 'onerous requirements' of s20. Three interviewees also stressed their philosophical dislike of using s20 to provide support care as accommodation under this section:

> [It negates the] whole spirit of the scheme which is being suggested [which] is about enabling parents, not removing power or disabling them if you like, which is why I think s17 is more appropriate.
>
> Lawyer, Authority L

Two out of three lawyers in authorities which do not operate support care noted that they would recommend using policies and procedures set in place by Link schemes (providing respite for disabled children) as a precedent for setting up a support care service, as they considered that the long-established nature of disability respite services would have ironed out potential problems to be faced in developing a new scheme.

A further two interviewees advised that they considered the Local Government Act 2002 (s1, 2 and 3) could be 'quite significant' when developing and promoting support services, as the 'general power to promote the well-being [of residents of an area] ... can be used to promote housing issues and provide accommodation, so that is another bit of legislation which seems to be in the same spirit'.

Issues of changes in legal status during support care placements

No lawyers expressed concerns about children moving from one legal status to another while accessing support care. Despite interviewees' reservations (see above) about the necessity for children to be looked after while using the service, the only examples of change of status which lawyers proposed involved cases where child protection concerns had arisen. No interviewees felt that this would prove problematic, as standard s47 enquiries would be instigated and (as suggested by two lawyers) children could remain placed with support carers while investigations were ongoing. One lawyer (in an authority without a scheme) felt strongly that services should be provided under s17 of the Children Act; their only concerns were centred on cases where a child spent increasing periods of time in respite care until it was clear that accommodation under s20 would have to be provided.

In the three authorities which offered support care, lawyers had no knowledge of complaints made against carers, or about the services offered.

Concerns over training/use of support carers as witnesses in child protection cases

Despite the potential conflict of interest which might exist where carers offered support to parents as well as providing accommodation for children, no lawyers indicated concerns over carers' reliability as witnesses, or the admissibility of their evidence in any care proceedings.

Similarly, interviewees did not generally feel that the fact support carers worked as 'part-time foster parents' – and might perhaps have less training than mainstream carers – would prove problematic in terms of quality of service offered, or if asked to appear as witnesses in any legal proceedings. Only one lawyer noted that in general, foster carers were 'kept out of court' in their area, but this was due to their lack of experience in such an arena.

Five out of six lawyers felt that as long as support carers were trained and assessed as foster carers, the quality of care offered to children in placement would be of a high enough standard to avoid any potential legal challenges or concerns. Only one interviewee expressed concerns over using childminders as support carers, but noted that if Ofsted regulations permitted childminders to offer overnight accommodation, the local authority would need to ensure that placements with such carers 'dovetail with the Children Act and the fostering regulations'.

Responsibility for providing leaving care packages to children accessing support care

In the main, informants felt that the Children (Leaving Care) Act 2000 would not apply in the case of young people who have been receiving support care (exemptions within the Act exclude pre-planned, 'respite' accommodation from being counted in the 13-week time limit). However, as noted throughout this report, some children using the scheme do move between support care and short-term accommodation depending upon the nature of their parents' difficulties (for example, parents with mental health issues may need to have their children placed in short-term accommodation from time to time) and local authority responsibilities therefore depend upon the individual child's situation.

However, three lawyers expressed some reservations about support for a vulnerable young person ending abruptly at the age of 16, and suggested that some form of compromise leaving care support might perhaps be available to children who are, or have recently been, in receipt of support care.

One interviewee, while noting that the potential existed to create an undue burden on local authorities by expecting them to offer a leaving care package to increased numbers of young people, felt that any review of legislation or regulations should include revisiting the exclusion on respite breaks. While not recommending that all young people who had received support care should be able to access the full leaving care package, this particular lawyer considered that a 'modified form' of entitlement should perhaps be available.

The remaining lawyers, however, while not favouring an extension to the Leaving Care Act duties (and in one case noting that this would prove a disincentive to authorities considering developing projects), commented that ongoing support could be provided through s17 (with, perhaps, strongly worded guidance to local authorities to remind them of their duties) or under the Local Government Act 2002 (see above).

> We have a very open-door system so offer packages to children who have had support … we exercise a lot of discretion [under the LGA 2002] to provide after-care for anyone who needs support and who falls outside the remit of children leaving care provisions.
>
> Lawyer, Authority C

Support care and performance management

Five of the six interviewees were able to comment positively in terms of both value to service users and cost-effectiveness of offering support care. In two cases explicit mention was made of 'added value' to families of offering children a stable home environment during placements, providing support to parents, and working to keep children at home.

Four informants felt that support care was 'good value for money' as 'a well-worked package can be cheaper, because the child doesn't go into full-time care'.

Two lawyers referred also to the fact that if s17 was used to offer the service, other benefits would accrue to both local authorities and service users, such as a reduction in the number of children recorded as looked after and hence an improvement in performance indicators; a strong message of support for the philosophy behind support care; less stigma for families receiving local authority accommodation; and lower investment of staff time in reviews and care planning.

Advice to authorities considering developing support care schemes

Legal and policy advisors in authorities currently operating support care schemes were asked if they had any specific recommendations to offer to colleagues asked to advise on setting up similar projects elsewhere.

Respondents to this question all stressed the importance of clear development of policies and procedures (including adequate training and safeguards), consideration of existing regulations, and exploring whether it was necessary to be 'locked into the full LAC procedures' which were regarded as time-consuming and overly bureaucratic for front-line staff.

Request for DH guidance

All respondents stressed that they would welcome receiving guidance on the operation and legal requirements of support care schemes from the Department of Health. Policy documents received from one authority, however, indicated that they felt LAC (2003) 13 provided adequate authority for the provision of support care through the route of s17 of the Children Act.

The most common response was a request for 'general guidance' on all aspects of support care. Informants who believed that neither s20 nor s17 of the Children Act offered a totally effective mechanism for provision of support care felt that advice was required on some form of hybrid legal status:

> Something on dealing with those packages which isn't s20 but then isn't really s17 either, because we need child protection issues built in. Need [to be able to] support in an s17 way, but the control and intrusiveness of s20 taken out and to limit the paperwork.
>
> Lawyer, Authority C

Other requests included clarification of Ofsted regulations and the ways in which they overlap with offering support care through childminders; explicit advice on the use of s17 to provide support care; information on 'the most appropriate legal status' of children accessing the service and ways of integrating paperwork to reduce the burden on social workers.

Most explicitly, one of the informants who requested that 'all aspects of the scheme [are] laid out in guidance' wished for information on:

> ... assessments, care planning for the child; proposed outcomes ... issues of meaningful participation [for child and family]; complaints procedures; assessment of carers; reviews; terminations of arrangements and police checking. Local authority lawyers are a crucial bit of these schemes so it is important to make sure that we have some guidance, not just for social workers.
>
> Lawyer, Authority L

Other

Finally, having considered issues of service user empowerment, one informant noted in passing that it might be possible for local authorities to explore the option of provision of support care services through Direct Payments to purchasers under the Children Act, on the grounds that:

> Direct Payments legislation is about people running their own show, making their own choices, and this scheme appears to fit within that, making their own respite arrangements, using it with someone who is approved, to make up their own package.
>
> Lawyer, Authority L